HEMINGWAY
&
The Sun Also Rises

Hemingway in the courtyard at 113 rue Notre Dame
des Champs, Paris, 1924 (photo no. 7239G, John F.
Kennedy Library)

HEMINGWAY

&

The Sun Also Rises

The Crafting of a Style

FREDERIC JOSEPH SVOBODA

UNIVERSITY PRESS OF KANSAS

All illustrations were obtained from the John F. Kennedy Library and are used here by permission of the Ernest Hemingway Foundation and Charles Scribner's Sons (for the jacket, reproduced in Chapter 6). Quotations from the unpublished works of Ernest Hemingway are by permission of Mrs. Mary Hemingway and the Ernest Hemingway Foundation and are copyrighted by Mrs. Mary Hemingway. Permission to reprint excerpts from the following works by Ernest Hemingway has been granted by Charles Scribner's Sons: *By-Line: Ernest Hemingway*—Copyright (c) 1967, Mary Hemingway; *In Our Time*—Copyright 1925 Charles Scribner's Sons; copyright renewed 1953 Ernest Hemingway; *A Moveable Feast*—Copyright (c) 1964 Ernest Hemingway, Ltd.; *The Nick Adams Stories*—Copyright (c) 1972 Ernest Hemingway Foundation; *The Sun Also Rises*—Copyright 1926 Charles Scribner's Sons; copyright renewed 1954 Ernest Hemingway. The letter of July 1926 from F. Scott Fitzgerald to Ernest Hemingway (see Appendix C) is reprinted from *Correspondence of F. Scott Fitzgerald,* ed. Matthew J. Brucolli and Margaret M. Duggan (New York: Random House, 1980), by permission of Random House, Inc.

Published by the University Press of Kansas (Lawrence, Kansas 66045), which was organized by the Kansas Board of Regents and is operated and funded by Emporia State University, Fort Hays State University, Kansas State University, Pittsburg State University, the University of Kansas, and Wichita State University.

Library of Congress Cataloging in Publication Data
Svoboda, Frederic Joseph, 1949–
  Hemingway & The sun also rises.
  Bibliography: p.
  Includes index.
  1. Hemingway, Ernest, 1899–1961. Sun also rises. 2. Hemingway, Ernest, 1899–1961—Style. 3. Hemingway, Ernest, 1899–1961—Criticism, Textual. I. Title. II. Title: Hemingway and The sun also rises.
PS3515.E37S93 1983   813'.52   82-20026
ISBN 0-7006-0228-3

$20

Printed in the United States of America

TO
MY PARENTS

Contents

List of Illustrations

Abbreviations Used in the Text

Works frequently referred to in the text are cited in abbreviated form in parentheses. Items in the Hemingway manuscript collection are identified by numbers corresponding to the collection's indexing system, explained in Appendix A. References to Hemingway's published books are abbreviated as follows:

iot	*in our time*, 1924
IOT	*In Our Time*, 1925
MF	*A Moveable Feast*, 1964
NAS	*The Nick Adams Stories*, 1972
SAR	*The Sun Also Rises*, 1926

Short forms used for secondary sources are:

Baker	Carlos Baker's *Ernest Hemingway: A Life Story*
Grebstein	Sheldon Norman Grebstein's *Hemingway's Craft*
PR	*Paris Review* interview with Hemingway, reprinted in Linda Wagner's *Ernest Hemingway: Five Decades of Criticism*
Reynolds	Michael Reynolds's *Hemingway's First War: The Making of a Farewell to Arms*
Sarason	Bertram D. Sarason's *Hemingway and The Sun Set*
Seldes	Gilbert Seldes's *Dial* review of *The Great Gatsby*
White	William White's *Byline: Ernest Hemingway*

1

Beginnings and Backgrounds

By July of 1925 it was time. Over a period of five years Ernest Miller Hemingway had already established a provisional reputation for himself as a writer of fresh, innovative prose. Returning home as a decorated war hero in 1919, he had soon begun to try to shape his experiences into prose fiction, first producing stories that proved only the promise of his talent. But gradually his career had moved forward.

Even as his stories were being rejected by magazines ranging from *Argosy* to the *Dial,* he had made himself a reputation as a journalist of clear and striking, though occasionally less than objective, style. He worked his way into Paris's literary set, helped to edit *Transatlantic Review,* a leading little magazine, and gained the attention of some of the prominent figures of the literary avant-garde of the day—and the prominent figures of a new literature that was then taking shape. Even a partial list of his friends and acquaintances is a roll call of modernism: Sherwood Anderson, Gertrude Stein, Ezra Pound, John Dos Passos, Ford Madox Ford, F. Scott Fitzgerald. By the mid twenties, his stories, now finely honed, attracted comment as they appeared in *Transatlantic Review* and *Contact.* Small editions of his stories and poems had been published in Paris, and a longer story collection, *In Our Time,* was about to appear in America. His reputation was rising, but its establishment required something more—it required that he write with mastery in the preeminent form, that of the novel.

In previous years he had twice traveled with friends to Pamplona, in Spain's Basque hill country, to join in the drinking and to run with the bulls during the Fiesta of San Fermin. But in this year, 1925, the fiesta was changing, becoming chic, a tourist attraction for foreigners who were not aficionados of the corrida.

Hemingway in the Spanish countryside, 1924 or 1925 (photo no. EH 7921P, John F. Kennedy Library)

And the beautiful trout stream that had provided a valued counterpoint of serenity to the frenzy of the fiesta had been ruined, clogged by the slashings and mud left behind after clear-cutting by loggers.

Hemingway's companions of 1925 had not turned out so well, either—they had too often been drunk and had too often come into conflict over one member of the party, Lady Duff Twysden. In the end, Duff and her lover, Pat Guthrie, had not even been able to pay their hotel bill, and the humorist Donald Ogden Stewart, one of the more amiable members of the party, had put up the money. The disappointments cut deep, but more than disappointments came out of the fiesta.

Stewart later wrote: "On the way from Pamplona to the [Gerald] Murphys in Antibes it occurred to me that the events of the past week might perhaps make interesting material for a novel. I was right. Ernest started work on *The Sun Also Rises* the next week" ("Recollections of Fitzgerald and Hemingway," *Fitzgerald/ Hemingway Annual, 1971,* pp. 185–86). Sometime around July fifteenth, Hemingway sat down to write; by September twenty-first he had completed the first draft of his novel, then tentatively titled *Fiesta.*

Apparently, Hemingway let the longhand manuscript of *Fiesta,* which now filled thirty-four loose sheets of paper plus seven stapled schoolchildren's notebooks, lie fallow. During the fall, again in a short period of time, he banged out *The Torrents of Spring,* the satiric short novel that allowed him to break his contract with publisher Horace Liveright. In the novel, Hemingway proclaimed his artistic independence from Sherwood Anderson, one of Liveright's star authors, who was the first major figure to become interested in Hemingway in Chicago in 1920. Naturally, Liveright declined a book satirizing Anderson, and Hemingway was free to offer his work to editor Maxwell Perkins of Scribner's.

By mid December, Hemingway, with his wife, Hadley, and their son, John, was cozily installed in the Hotel Taube in Schruns, Austria. The change of publishers necessitated a trip to New York; but in spite of that trip and the blossoming of his love affair with Pauline Pfeiffer, who was to be his second wife, Hemingway returned to Schruns. It was a year of avalanches, and Hemingway spent long hours away from the ski slopes, working over his manuscript, first marking changes between the lines and in the margins of the notebooks and loose sheets, sometimes canceling five or six pages with big inked *X*s, and later typing out experimental beginnings. Finally he typed out a new draft, changing the novel to a straight chronological organization rather than its earlier beginning *in medias res,* removing many sections in which the novel's narrator had addressed his reader directly, and carefully changing the names of those characters who might easily have been confused with their real-life prototypes.

Back in Paris a typist produced a clear copy of his awkwardly spaced typescript. After making some further emendations in difficult scenes, Hemingway sent the novel off to Scribner's, his new publisher. Copy editors worked over the typescript. Then, at the suggestion of Scott Fitzgerald, who read a copy of the typescript, Hemingway removed most of the first two chapters, which had begun, "This is a novel about a Lady"—Lady Brett Ashley. He tried to write a short introduction to explain the disappearance of those chapters, but finally he just began with a line partway through the deleted second chapter: "Robert Cohn was middleweight boxing champion of Princeton."

By mid October of 1926 *The Sun Also Rises* had reached the bookstores, and by Christmas it was into its third printing. Critics generally praised it as a work of remarkable stature; the reviewer in the *New York Times Book Review* called it "magnificent writing, filled with that organic action which gives a compelling picture of character" (31 October 1926, p. 7). Hemingway was no longer a promising new face but a man who had accomplished a great deal and of whom much could yet be expected. His reputation was established.

A new style and technique had arrived in American writing. In fashioning *The Sun Also Rises*, Hemingway had both followed and shaped a set of principles that he was to follow and elucidate for the rest of his life, principles that could not be ignored, whether they were to be followed or not, by any serious writer who came after him. Recently, the manuscripts and typescripts of Hemingway's writing have been made available to scholars; therefore the development of *The Sun Also Rises* can be carefully elucidated and tracked in these materials, which are deposited in the Hemingway Collection of the John F. Kennedy Library and in the Manuscripts Department of the University of Virginia's Alderman Library. Ernest Hemingway solidified the principles of a new kind of fiction as he crafted and honed the prose of *The Sun Also Rises*. Here are the steps he followed in reshaping the form.

2

From Journalism to Fiction

Following a classic technique of the short story, Hemingway began the first draft of *The Sun Also Rises,* not at the chronological beginning of the novel's action, in late June in Paris's Montparnasse, but with an event near the climax of the novel's plot line and with a character who was central to the meaning of the story. The character is a young matador, and the event is his meeting with two Americans. The place is the matador's cramped hotel room as he dresses for the bullring. The scene is followed by a conversation between the Americans and a Spanish aficionado of the bullfight, an argument between a Scotsman and an American, and the arrival in the town square—in all his banal glory—of the American ambassador.

Anyone familiar with *The Sun Also Rises* will immediately identify the characters and the action. The characters of the first scene must be Pedro Romero, Jake Barnes, and Bill Gorton. The Spanish aficionado is Montoya, owner of the hotel, and the ensuing argument is between Robert Cohn and Mike Campbell, in response to Brett Ashley's appreciative remarks about Romero. All this is happening on Monday July 7, the second day of Pamplona's Fiesta of San Fermin.

But a close examination—or even a cursory one—of this beginning will reveal many differences between this draft and the published novel. In the novel, most obviously, Hemingway begins to present this material, not on page 1, but on page 163. The matador of the first draft is not Romero but Cayetano Ordoñez, nicknamed "Niño de la Palma." The American who is telling the story is addressed, not as Jake, but as Hem or Ernest, and the others are called by their real names, which would be unfamiliar to those who know only Hemingway's works of fiction: Pat, Don, Harold, Duff, and Hadley. Cayetano Ordoñez was a highly

5

(1)

Cayetano Ordoñez
"Niño de la Palma"

I saw him for the first time in his room at the Hotel Quintana in Pamplona. Quintana We met Quintana on the stairs as Bill and I were coming up to the room to get the wine bag to take to the bull fight. comida. "Come on," said Quintana. "Would you like to meet Niño de la Palma?" He was in room number eight, I knew what it was like inside, a gloomy room with the two beds separated by monastic partitions. Bill had lived in there room and gotten out to take a single room when the fiesta started. Quintana knocked and opened the door. He introduced us. The boy stood very straight and unsmiling in his white shirt and green pants he was dressed all except his coat and his hair had just been wound. He nodded seeming far away unsmiling and dignified when we shook hands. Quintana made a little speech about what great aficionados we were and how we wanted to wish him luck. Niño turned to me. He was the best looking kid I have ever seen. "You go to see the bull fight," he said in English

First page of the earliest draft of *The Sun Also Rises:* the meeting between Bill and the narrator and the matador—here named Cayetano Ordonez, ''Niño de la Palma'' (193-1)

(7)

taking any man away after he has passed a
certain age.

Well they stood out there on the
sidewalk and a crowd gathered to look at
the car and a policeman Every body in the café
who had taken a good look at them and was
either drinking back to drinking again all except
us that is. Duff said, "I say. That's a
shabby way to treat an Ambassador." Don
said, "But he's only an American Ambassador."
Bill said, "They don't know that here though."
"Go on Hem," Duff said. "You know him. Go
out and give him the keys of the city say
something to him."
"Give him the keys of the city," Pat said.
"Give him the key to my room," Don said.
"Go on Hem You really ought," Duff said.

Page 7 of the first draft of *The Sun Also Rises*, an apparently journalistic
account that included the names of real people: [Lady] Duff [Twysden], Don
[Stewart], Bill [Smith], Pat [Guthrie], and Hem [himself] (193-7)

On page 31 of the first draft, the names of real people, including [Harold] Loeb and Hadley [Richardson Hemingway] were still being used by Hemingway. They soon began to disappear as the process of fictionalization proceeded rapidly (193-31).

regarded young matador of the 1925 season, and the others are easily recognizable as real people: the bankrupt Pat Guthrie; the writer of best-selling humorous novels Donald Ogden Stewart; Harold Loeb, a novelist and the scion of a wealthy Jewish-American family; Lady Duff Twysden, a British member of the smart international set; and Hemingway's first wife, Hadley Richardson Hemingway. Also mentioned is Bill Smith, an old friend who had often hunted and fished with Hemingway in Michigan. Later, John Dos Passos, Ford Madox Ford, and F. Scott Fitzgerald appeared. What we are witnessing in the thirty-two handwritten pages of the novel's original beginning seems to be something very close to journalism, if not a completely journalistic account of Hemingway's 1925 trip to Spain.

Of course, it has never been a secret that *The Sun Also Rises* is a *roman à clef;* when the novel first appeared, members of the expatriate literary community did not have to expend much energy in matching characters to real people, yet what is striking when one examines the first draft is not how journalistic it is but how quickly it moves away from a simple recounting of events. The change is perhaps most obvious in regard to the characters. As Hemingway's round, bold handwriting moves on from the thirty-two loose pages into the first of seven notebooks that hold the rest of the original draft, journalism rapidly turns to fiction. Only partway into the first notebook the narrator is no longer Hem (indeed, on only three pages of the rough draft are there references to Hemingway as the narrator) but Jake, and by page 39 of the notebook, that masterful and much discussed narrative device, Jake's war wound, has already been introduced, although nowhere in the manuscripts is it any more clearly identified than in the published novel. At about the same point the character of Bill is synthesized by a melding of traits of Don Stewart and Bill Smith. Hadley soon disappears as a character, and by the last notebook of the first draft, all characters save Duff have acquired fictional names, though not necessarily the names they will eventually bear in the finished novel.

A number of memoirs have considered the parallels between the actual participants in Hemingway's 1925 trip and the characters of the novel. These include works by Kathleen Cannell (''Frances Clyne''), Donald Ogden Stewart (''Bill Gorton''), Harold Loeb (''Robert Cohn''), and others. Recently, Bertram Sarason, in *Hemingway and the Sun Set,* has brought together selections from these memoirs and considered the *roman à clef* in detail. Each of these works makes a significant contribution to an understanding of what Hemingway was about, but such treatments also tend to overemphasize the *roman à clef* and to lead to a significant misinterpretation of Hemingway's real achievement in *The Sun Also Rises.* They often point out the inaccuracies of Hemingway's presentation of the trip, and sometimes they portray the novel as a betrayal of confidences exchanged between trusted friends. This latter attiude is most poignantly seen in the writings of Loeb; in a *Connecticut Review* article (''Hemingway's Bitterness''), later reprinted in Sarason's work, Loeb conveyed the essence of this position: ''Nothing in our relationship justified the distortion of the real friend that I was into the Robert Cohn of *The Sun Also Rises*'' (Sarason, p. 134). Loeb's pain is clear and certainly is not to be dismissed lightly, yet he cannot know how Hemingway transformed his material, or why.

What these writers are missing, quite naturally given that they feel abused, is that Hemingway was not interested in a literal transcription from reality. Indeed, those sections of the first draft that were most literally true to what happened in Paris and Pamplona—those most closely journalistic or autobiographical—tended to be cut as Hemingway revised. Thus, an encounter between Dos Passos and Ford was cut out, though much of it later appeared (minus Dos Passos) as the chapter of

Hemingway's memoir *A Moveable Feast* in which Ford mistakes the diabolist Aleister Crowley for the poet Hilaire Belloc. The material was suitable for a memoir yet was not sufficiently fictionalized to meet Hemingway's standard for the transformation of real material into the novel form.

Writing years later, in an unpublished draft for *A Moveable Feast,* Hemingway introduced a term to describe this transformation: "inventing from experience." He acknowledged his debts but also discounted the confusion of reality and fiction: "When you first start writing stories in the first person if the stories are made so real that people believe them the people reading them nearly always think the stories really happened to you. . . . In the early days writing in Paris I would invent not only from my own experience but from the experiences and knowledge of my friends and all the people I had known or met since I could remember who were not writers" (179-1).* In the mention of inventing from experience, Hemingway reminds us of something that is too easy to forget once we begin tracing the relationship of real people to fictional characters—namely, that *The Sun Also Rises* is not a flawed work of journalism but is superbly realized fiction. If a certain trip to Pamplona helped to provide a framework for that fiction, that is all well and good. But the framework was altered and adapted as the novel took shape, and the fictional creation was thus distanced form the historical/journalistic fact.

* Throughout this work, insofar as possible, the actual spellings and punctuation used by Hemingway in his drafts are reproduced. Except in rare cases, the use of *sic* has been avoided as being intrusive. These are drafts and should not be expected to exhibit the perfection of a final edited text. Similarly, Hemingway's editing has been preserved. Where he crossed out a word, the word is printed and lined through. Where he added words, these words are in italics.

3

The Iceberg:
Hemingway's Notes to Himself

Much of the material that Hemingway presented early in his first draft was later altered considerably in style, moved to other locations within the novel, or even omitted entirely. Yet this deleted material is vital to the development of his finished work. In these beginnings, Hemingway was clearly staking out major thematic considerations: the ways in which experience has shaped him and his generation, the sorts of values that are worth upholding, and those values that must be rejected as useless. Hemingway's working out of these questions was direct and sometimes intensely personal. Thematic elements that he eventually integrated carefully into the structure of the novel were clearly discussed as Hemingway first worked to develop his ideas. Given the characteristic restraint with which he tried to handle such material, it was inevitable that he later would choose to make considerable revisions and deletions as he reworked this early material. Such changes would be needed less often in the revision of later sections of the first draft, after Hemingway had already clearly defined what he was attempting to do.

To use Hemingway's own image, discussed in the *Paris Review* interview, *The Sun Also Rises* has the solidity of an iceberg, seven-eighths unseen yet carefully based on that early, unseen foundation. Early in the first draft—most particularly in the loose sheets and the first notebook—some of the submerged foundation of the novel can be clearly seen. In the voice of the narrator, Jake Barnes, not yet wholly differentiated from Hemingway's own voice, he often speaks directly in order to explain his artistic intentions or to insert material that is important to the working out of those intentions.

Early in the first notebook, Hemingway began to consider his plans for the book. He hoped to write a new sort of prose that would derive from the language and facts of real life, yet he was conscious that such a method would call for a discerning and careful reader:

> In life people are not conscious of these special moments that novelists build their whole structures on. That is most people are not. That surely has nothing to do with the story but you can not tell until you finish it because none of the significant things are going to have any literary signs marking them. You have to figure them out by yourself. [194-1-9]

Hemingway was not saying that he intended to be careless about structure; rather, he was very much opposed to an artificially imposed conventional structure. He was seeking to remove the conventional frameworks interposed between the reader and the reality that is represented in a work of art. By eliminating the "literary signs," he hoped to move beyond the existing conventions of literary art and the existing conventions of middle-class thought that were both familiar and confining to him.

A few pages before his renunciation of conventional literary signs, Hemingway seemed to be working out that renunciation as he presented an incident in which a conventional frame might have obscured or distorted the reality of the situation he was describing. The scene, a memory scene involving the narrator's family, is splendidly comic though perhaps a little too neat. The narrator remembers the death of his namesake uncle, whose funeral he had attended with his mother. In the scene, the little boy is repeatedly warned about a number of minor vices he should avoid and then is told how those vices led to the downfall of his deceased uncle. The narrator (Jake or Hemingway—the two have not yet become clearly differentiated—and in the manuscript, Hemingway tried Raphael Ernest and Jake as names for him) remembers that "there were ~~many~~ several things my mother said she would rather see me in my grave than do. They were quite unimportant things such as smoking cigarettes, gambling, and drinking and the last two were quite unthought of ~~sins~~ and far off sins" (194-1-7).

The tone of the mother's warning doesn't quite square with the boy's memories of his uncle, who gave wonderful Christmas gifts, owned the first car in town, sponsored civic entertainments, including a horse show, and organized "sinister things known as French Fetes on his grounds for the benefit of the local hospital" (194-1-7). Arriving late at the funeral and being seated in the front row, the boy wonders what they had done with his uncle until he suddenly sees, "in the midst of the mass of flowers the high, gallant, hooked purple nose of Uncle ~~Raphael~~ Jacob." He is "frozen with an absolutely new sensation all through the rest of the funeral, afraid to look and unable to look away from that majestic, cold purple nose" (194-1-8).

Young Jacob cannot overlook the reality of his uncle's death; his reaction to the death is juxtaposed by Hemingway to the mother's attitude, The boy thinks about his mother's statement that she would rather see him dead than at all morally tainted, and he wonders why she would wish him to end that way rather than

The ~~first matador got the horn through his hand~~ *Bull got the first Matador through the sword hand* and the

crowd hooted him ~~and~~ *out* the second matador slipped and the

bull caught him through the ~~xxxxxx~~ *belly* and he hung onto the

horn ~~and xxxxxx~~ with one hand and held the other tight against the

place and ~~it xxxxxx~~ *the bull tossed him and then the horn came out* *wildeyed* and he lay in the sand and then g~~o~~t up/and *cried*

slugged the men that tried to carry him away and ~~xxxxxx~~ for his

sword but he fainted/. *and they carried him off.* The kid came out and had to kill five bulls

~~xxix the last xxx xxxxxxxx~~ *because* *only* xyou can/have three matadors for the day

and the last bull he killed he was so tired he couldn't get the

sword in ~~x~~ He tried five times and finally got it through and the

cpowd ~~xxxxxxxxxxxxxxxxxxxxxxxxxxxx~~ *was quiet all the time waiting and never razzed him* . Then they raised

hell when he finally put it through and the bull went down .

Immmmmmmthhxgmmmmbmmbmxxxmmm

Unwritten Stories .

I remember riding along in the dark and the whole battery

was drunk . Everybody was drunk going along thxxxxhxxhxxdxxkx

the road in the dark .The Lieutenant kept riding his horse out

into the fields and saying/,"I'm drunk I tell you mon vieux .Oh *to him .,*

Ikm je suis fou ." We went along the road all night in the dark and

the adjutant was very drunk and I had a fire in my kitchen and

he kept riding up alongside and saying ," You must put it out . It

is dangerous . It will be observed . " We were thirty kilometers

from the front and the further/we got the more he worried .} *away*

Imxxxmkxxxchenxxxxxpxxxhxxhxmxxmxxxxmxxxxxgxxmgxxxxhxxhxmxxxxhxxxxmg

ximxthe Champagnm

It was very funny going drunk along that road in the dark . I was

kitchen corporal then and we were going to entrain for the Champagne.

Two of what became the chapters of *In Our Time*. Notice that here Hemingway called them ''Unwritten Stories,'' perhaps evoking his idea of the iceberg, where seven-eighths of a story is unseen, yet felt (92).

commit any of several minor sins. The narrator considers the inadequacy of a moral framework within which the mother could express such a wish—and he links the wish, by implication, to an inadequate use of language. The mother's moral vision is inadequate at least partly because its expression is not suitable to the sentiment; it lacks restraint and grace. If the mother believes what she literally says, she is a monster; if, as is far more likely, she means something very different from her literal statement, she is guilty of falsification or foolish confusion.

In his formulation of this childhood event—whether fictional or autobiographical—Hemingway linked the moral and the aesthetic, much as he had done in earlier work. In her clouded vision, the mother of this anecdote is like the unseeing characters of many of the chapters of *In Our Time*. In that collection an adjutant in World War I wants the fire doused in a mobile field kitchen because "it is dangerous. It will be observed," even though the kitchen is fifty kilometers behind the front lines (*IOT*, p. 13); and a British officer discusses a barricade set across a bridge and the resulting slaughter of troops trying to cross—"It was simply priceless. . . . It was an absolutely perfect obstacle." The officer's only emotions result, not from a contemplation of the dead, but from the loss of other positions, which forces a withdrawal and an end to the sport of killing: "We were frightfully put out" (*IOT*, p. 43). A young man under bombardment in the trenches prays that he may not be killed; if he lives, he will "tell everybody in the world that you are the only thing that matters. Please, please, dear Jesus" (*IOT*, p. 87). And then, when he is saved, he is too ashamed to tell anyone anything. A policeman murders two burglars without warning; and then he discounts his partner's suggestion that the murders might cause touble: "They're wops, ain't they? Who the hell is going to make any trouble?" (*IOT*, p. 103). But though the murderer-policeman protests his ability to spot them "a mile off," the two dead men are not "wops" but Hungarians.

None of these characters really knows or means what he says. Each uses language in ways that are foolish, insensitive, shameful, or inaccurate. Their shoddy use of language is not clear or aesthetic or moral. And in his discussion of the mother's inadequate expression of her thoughts and the little boy's fearful, troubled reaction, Hemingway was stating his opposition to shoddy expression and reaffirming his commitment to a clear, carefully crafted prose that would avoid all misstatement. Even thirty some years later, Hemingway contended that "writing well is impossibly difficult" (*PR*, p. 27). Yet "writing well" was precisely what Hemingway intended to do, even though the task of doing so in a work the length of a novel was more than a little imposing and risky. In *A Moveable Feast* he recalls that "it seemed an impossible thing to do when I had been trying with great difficulty to write paragraphs that would be the distillation of what made a novel" (*MF*, p. 75).

Writing well was "impossibly difficult" precisely because Hemingway, in his fiction, effected a close linking of both moral and aesthetic principles. And a reader's understanding of the aesthetics of his fiction will be necessary to an understanding of other levels of meaning—including the moral level—without the aid of more "conventional literary signs." In the first draft of *The Sun Also Rises*, particularly early in the first draft, Hemingway continually experimented with implied meaning, as he did in the often chilling misstatements of the chapters of *In Our Time*, and as he did in the anecdote about the mother and the child. In the anecdote and in later trials he was at once exploring and reaffirming a method and a judgment.

Throughout his first draft, Hemingway continued to explore the morality and aesthetics of language. Later, as he revised *The Sun Also Rises*, he cut out such authorial discussions completely, as he did with another important section, corresponding to the published chapter 12, the chapter in which Jake and Bill have gone off away from the turmoil of the group to fish the Irati and the Río de la Fábrica, near Burguete.

It should be noted that the description of Jake and Bill's fishing trip has been carefully included in the novel, not as a part of the sort of journalistic account that the novel has sometimes been viewed as, but for reasons that are important to the overall effect it will have in juxtaposition to other actions of the characters. A purely journalistic description of the events of June 1925 would have been far different from the idyllic week of relaxation that Hemingway described. In previous years the fishing had been ideal, but in 1925 Bill Smith, Donald Ogden Stewart, and Hemingway found that the fishing had been ruined by the logging of the beech and pine forests. Carlos Baker describes the ruin:

> The dark stream bed of the Irati was filled with loggers' trash. "The irony of it," said Don Stewart. "The pity of it." They put away the flies and used worms and grasshoppers, working along the Río Fábrica and some of the smaller streams. In four days of trying, they did not take a single fish. "Fish killed, pools destroyed, dams broken down," said Ernest. "Made me feel sick." [Baker, p. 149]

From the general ruin, it appears that Hemingway salvaged only the contrast between fishing with bait and fishing with flies, and Stewart's comment on irony and pity. The rest of the chapter appears to owe far more to Hemingway's previous fishing experience and to his need for a suitable section to work in contrast to his evocation of a morally squalid Paris and a frenetic Pamplona at fiesta time.

In the initial draft of the fishing at Burguete, Hemingway was already working to develop a clear-cut opposition—the draft contains no hint that in 1925 Burguete was surrounded by a ruined country. Within the first-draft version of this chapter, Hemingway also returned to the consideration of the kind of fiction he was writing, working through a comparison hardly so organic to the structure of the novel as is the Paris/Pamplona/Burguete juxtaposition. In a set-piece discussion, Jake considers a story he is reading (*SAR*, p. 120).

Jake and Bill finish lunch; then Bill falls asleep, and Jake goes on to think of A. E. W. Mason's story "The Crystal Trench," which he had been reading earlier,

Say Palmer. It was funny about the glacier. Why did not some one write some good Mountain stories. ~~the~~ ~~of~~ ~~writer~~ went there. One ~~never~~ ~~the~~ ~~talked of~~ ~~them~~ thought of a glacier the snow blowing and the ~~snow~~ blown clean off and the ~~ice~~ ~~was~~ ~~hard~~ ~~blown~~ ~~clean~~ ~~off~~ out a blue glare ~~in the~~ ~~moonlight.~~ ~~It~~ clouded over and the glacier was dark and you could not see the ice for the snow blowing. We brought it down a dead German with a rope around him. His wife was down in the club hut waiting for everybody to come down to happen. The avalanche had not treated him like Mark Frobisher. When we dug him out he was ~~together~~ ~~off~~ ~~Frobisher~~ He had ~~been~~ ~~pretty~~ ~~well~~ ~~frozen~~ ~~but~~ ~~him~~ had been mixed up with him and why. We started down with him and Sometimes we hauled him out and

Sometimes we let him slide or ahead. Down below was the hut with snow blowing around it. When we came in ~~out~~ of the hut I went on ahead to get a blanket. At the end tunnel the inside the ~~shutters~~ ~~were~~ ~~shut~~ ~~The~~ windows of the hut were shuttered ~~shutters~~ ~~were~~ were up. As I came around the corner I saw his wife inside the hut ~~twenty~~ ~~little~~ ~~just~~ ~~by~~ ~~the~~ little window. She was ~~Münchenkind~~ his Socha. I put the skis against the wall of the hut and opened the door and went in. The caretaker was cutting wood in the entry way. I opened the inner door and went in. His wife looked up. I saw she was disappointed it was me. "Heil," she said. I went on into the Waschraum

"Why did not some one write some good mountain stories." Hemingway wrote a mountain story more realistic than, though perhaps just as ironic as, A. E. W. Mason's. Hemingway cut this material, probably because it distracted the reader from the present events of *The Sun Also Rises* (194-4-13).

and he retells the story from memory. In the story, a man freezes to death in the Alps, his body falls into a glacial crevasse, "and his bride was going to wait 24 years exactly for his body to come out on the moraine, while her true love waited too" (194-4-12). Jake analyzes Mason's story, with particular attention to the predictabililty of its sequence of events. Indeed, to Jake the only thing that makes the story worth reading is its predictability. In the resolution to the story, as Jake retells it in considerable detail, the waiting bride discovers a locket around the neck of the corpse, which has reappeared just on schedule, twenty-four years after dropping into the glacier. She opens the locket and discovers—of course—the name of another woman. The twenty-four year wait has been a vain gesture.

To the romantically unrealistic account of this ridiculous story, Jake compares a far different story—a "true" story that also involves the Alps and a husband and wife. The contrast is striking: the story that Jake tells might have been used by Hemingway as a part of *In Our Time,* had it been written earlier. Jake has been skiing in the Austrian Alps. A man is killed in a sudden avalanche, and Jake is among those who recover the body and carry it down from the mountainside. Jake walks into the lodge, past the dead man's unsuspecting wife, who is darning a spare pair of his socks, to find a blanket with which to cover the corpse before it is brought in.

The story that Jake tells is infinitely better than Mason's story, although it parallels that story in the use of an ironic ending twist for emotional impact. Jake's story, though it is not so sensational, contains some of the horror of the later Hemingway story "An Alpine Idyll," in which a mountaineer stores his wife's body in the woodshed, using it as a lantern stand until the spring thaw makes burial possible. But Jake's story is far different from Mason's: Jake's is tersely realistic whereas Mason's is easily sentimental. In juxtaposition, the two stories demonstrate not only the sort of fiction that Hemingway hoped to avoid but also the sort that he valued.

By the second draft, Hemingway had chosen to remove all traces of Jake's tightly told story about the avalanche, and he had reduced Mason's story to a short mention, leaving the focus of the chapter on the two fishermen's experiences in Burguete rather than moving outside that framework. In place of the contrast between the two stories—one contrived, the other realistic—Hemingway extended the comic discussion between Jake and Bill, beginning with a verbal parody of William Jennings Bryan and going on to discuss a number of contemporary personages, including the Episcopal bishop William Thomas Manning, who called for a fundamentalist interpretation of scripture and who favored prohibition, and Wayne B. Wheeler of the Anti-Saloon League, both of whom were notable misusers of the langauge, at least from the point of view of the imbibing Jake and Bill.

Jake and Bill's discussion of these personalities in a bantering conversation allowed Hemingway to suggest the fraudulent uses of language in an organic manner that is at once more subtle ("none of the significant things are going to have any literary signs marking them'') and less obtrusive upon the novel's present time on the river than the long discussion in the stories would have allowed. The revision by substitution, by the way, is quite similar to the method used by Hemingway in completing his long short story "Big Two-Hearted River," one of the most thoroughly revised of Hemingway's early pieces, to judge from the manuscript evidence. In that story, which also involves an emotionally and physically scarred fisherman, Nick Adams, Hemingway originally broke away from his presentation of Nick's fishing in the Upper Peninsula of Michigan to end with a long discussion of the meaning of writing and what he intended to do with the story. The manuscript of that story is the only surviving Hemingway material, previous to the drafts of *The Sun Also Rises,* which shows the sort of working out of ideas on paper that so marks the novel's early drafts. Like the early sections of the novel, this early ending to the story speaks directly of Hemingway's experiences in expatriate literary society, when he was evaluating the work of Donald Ogden Stewart, E. E. Cummings, Ring Lardner, Sherwood Anderson, Gertrude Stein, Nathan Asch, James Joyce, and others.

As at the beginning of the first draft of *The Sun Also Rises,* in this early draft of "Big Two-Hearted River" the separation between author and narrator has not yet been clearly established. Nick Adams is perhaps the most nearly autobiographical of Hemingway's heroes, and in the original ending to the story, Nick speaks directly of Hemingway's friends, his enthusiasm for bullfighting and painting, and even his theory of writing:

> Talking about anything was bad. Writing about anything actual was bad. It always killed it.
> The only writing that was any good was what you made up, what you imagined. . . . Everything good he'd ever written he'd made up. None of it had ever happened. Other things had happened. Better things, maybe. That was what the family couldn't understand. They thought it all was experience. [*NAS*, pp. 237-38]

In this original ending to "Big Two-Hearted River," which was published in 1972 under the title "On Writing" in *The Nick Adams Stories,* Hemingway went on to make the important point that even with this, his most nearly autobiographical character, "Nick in the stories was never himself. He made him up" (*NAS*, p. 238). And the idea that "talking about anything . . . always killed it" first appeared in print in the ending of *The Sun Also Rises,* as Jake and Brett sit in the bar of the Palace Hotel, discussing Romero's love for Brett—very carefully:

> ". . . He thinks it was me. Not the show in general" [says Brett].
> "Well, it was you."
> "Yes. It was me."
> "I thought you weren't going to ever talk about it."
> "How can I help it?"
> "You'll lose it if you talk about it."
> "I just talk around it." [*SAR*, p. 245]

18

There the statement of artistic principle was carefully worked into the fabric of the novel, while it was not well integrated into the sensuous flow of "Big Two-Hearted River." In revising the long story, Hemingway began again at the point where he had begun to stray from the clear movement of action (at the end of the partial paragraph at the top of p. 208 of *In Our Time,* where Nick thinks of the difficulty of fishing upstream in a heavy current). From that point he wrote the familiar ending in a draft that required almost no revision, carefully keeping to the framework he had established earlier. Similarly, the first draft of Jake's discussion of the two Alpine stories was not integrated into *The Sun Also Rises,* and the story he tells might more appropriately have been added to the extended characterization of a Nick Adams—the image of Jake Barnes as an Alpine skier would have intruded into the structure of the novel. In the first draft, Jake was carefully established as a trustworthy expert in many areas that are organic to the movement of the novel. Alpine skiing has nothing to do with what happens to the novel's characters in Paris, Pamplona, San Sebastián, Hendaye, or Madrid, and it might logically have been eliminated as Hemingway tightened his drafts.

In a 1958 interview in the *Paris Review,* Hemingway restated one of the primary principles at work in his early fiction—a principle that he consistently followed throughout his career: "I always try to write on the principle of the iceberg. There is seven eighths of it under water for every part that shows. Anything you know you can eliminate and it only strengthens your iceberg" (p. 35). Like Hemingway's emphasis on not "killing" or "losing" things, this statement on the value of submerged knowledge seems to derive from a belief in careful artistic control, a commitment to a high degree of artistic craftsmanship, and a strong belief that fiction must be far more than simple journalsism. This is not merely a commitment to "art for art's sake," though certainly Hemingway always strove for artistic perfection, but also a result of the conviction that only in a carefully controlled and crafted art can searching, truthful insight be achieved. In speaking of characterization, he exemplified this conviction in the *Paris Review:* "If you describe someone, it is flat, as a photograph is, and from my standpoint a failure. If you make him up from what you know, there should be all the dimensions" (p. 35).

Within Hemingway's framework of artistic intention, the thing that is left out may be almost as important as that which is left in. In particular, even such masked authorial intrusions as Jake's memory of his uncle's funeral and Jake's analysis of A. E. W. Mason's story are suspect. In Hemingway's view, explanations may be eliminated or substantially reduced; explanation is never so truthful as direct presentation; and journalistic presentation is never so complete as the artist's invention from his knowledge of the world. William Carlos Williams might have been speaking for Hemingway, as he was struggling to shape *The Sun Also Rises,* when Williams stated his own prime artistic principle, the imagistic "no ideas but in things."

Within a framework that relies on the reader's ability to perceive the "significant things" (194-1-9) and their relationships within the novel, explana-

Chapter Sixteen .

I do not know what time I got to bed . I remember undressing , putting on a bath robe and standing out on the balcony . I knew I was quite drunk and when I came in I put on the light over the head of the bed and started to read . I was reading a book by Turgenieff . Probably I read the same two pages over several times . It was one of the stories in A Sportsman's Sketches . I had read it before but it seemed quite new . The country became very clear and the feeling of pressure in my head seemed to loosen . I was very drunk and I did not want to shut my eyes because the room would go round and round . If I kept on reading that/would pass . *feeling*

I heard Brett and Robert Cohn come up the stairs . R Cohn said good night outside the door and went on up to his room . I heard Brett go into the room next door . Mike was already in bed . He had come in with me an hour before . He woke as she came in and they talked together . I heard them laugh . I turned off the light and tried to go to sleep . It was not necessary to read anymore . I could shut my eyes without getting the wheeling sensation . But I could not sleep .

And the conversation of all day kept coming back in a sort of regurgitation . I felt pretty well through with Brett . In life you tried to go along with out criticising the actions of other people but sometimes they offended you in spite of yourself. Brett had lost something . Since she had gone to San Sebastian with Cohn she seemed to have lost that quality in her that had never been touched before . All this talking now about former lovers to make this seem quite ordinary . She was ashamed . That was it . She had never been ashamed before . It made her vulgar where before she had been simply going by her own rules . She had wanted to kill off something in her

An explanation of Jake's feelings for Brett. This material (above and on facing page) is typical of what Hemingway cut precisely because it explained too much (198-2-1 and 2).

and the killing had gotten out of her control . Well she had killed it
off in me . That was a good thing . I did not want to be in love with any
woman . I did not want to have any grand passion that I could never do
anything about . I was glad it was gone . The hell I was .

It had been gone for years really . There shall refxxi Something Something
of it had always been there though . There had been a time when I had
loved her so much   that it seemed there was nothing else in the world .
That there could be nothing more ever never be anything else . The world
was all one dimensional and flat and there was nothing but Brett   and
wanting Brett . I killed that off with my head . That was when she
had married Ashley . Every time I thought of Brett I deliberately thought
of her with Ashley . This with Ashley . That with Ashley . Sir Robert
Ashley . Lord Robert Ashley . That made two Roberts for her .

It was funny that as I killed off the love for Brett
the world began to come back . It wasn't flat anymore . Gradually it
all came back . Perhaps it was simply that my health cleared around
. Maybe it was . Anyway when I looked back on making myself hate Brett
it seemed sophomoric and wartime and silly . Then when she left
Ashley and came to Paris with Michael she took it for granted that I
still loved her . And I found that I had not killed it off at all .
I guess I could never kill it off while she was away . It would have to
be killed while she was there or it wouldn't last stay dead .

I was all straightened out inside now and I could take it .
I could take a hell of a lot now . Because the world did not go flat on
me anymore . Loving Brett could hurt me now but it couldn't hurt me
much . I could see the whole show pretty clearly now . I was probably
lucky that I was not whole and well . That seemed a rotten way to look
at it compared with the heroics I used to work up in nineteen sixteen
and seventeen but it was a more comfortable feeling . Of course I still

tions must be suspect. Such fraudulent preaching as the mother's in the funeral anecdote moves neither the writer nor the reader closer to a direct, unobstructed perception of the author's multidimensional reality. Even the most accurate expository section cannot compare in flexibility and effect to a more direct presentation through invention; explanation cannot evoke the complex of emotions and associations that is possible in direct presentation to an alert reader. Writing in *A Moveable Feast* about the early development of his methods, Hemingway noted that his starting point, when writing seemed difficult or impossible, was to "write one true sentence, and then go on from there. . . . If I started to write elaborately, or like someone introducing or presenting something, I found that I could cut that scrollwork or ornament out and throw it away and start with the first true simple declarative sentence I had written" (*MF*, p. 12). Yet the aim of Hemingway's simple declarative sentence is not intended to be a simple reading experience. He aims, not for the simplicity of a McGuffy reader, but for the apparent simplicity of a Manet, a Monet, or a Cézanne. In *A Moveable Feast,* he carefully qualified the place of simplicity in his art, using the work of the Impressionists as a touchstone for judging his effects: "I was learning something from the painting of Cézanne that made writing simple true sentences far from enough to make the stories have the dimensions that I was trying to put in them. I was learning very much from him" (p. 13). Hemingway worked to convey a multidimensional truth with apparent simplicity. And within such a framework of apparent simplicity, extended comments and explanations, though functional in the working out of the novel, serve best when subordinated or consigned to their place in the novel's foundation, in the unseen supporting bulk of the iceberg.

4
Narration and the Developing Shape of the Novel

While *The Sun Also Rises* is a tight, carefully crafted novel, Hemingway found it necessary to rework his early drafts considerably before the novel achieved a shape acceptable to him. In *A Moveable Feast* he recalled the extreme difficulty of shaping the novel from his first draft; the revision was accomplished during his winter of skiing in Austria, after Hemingway had quickly completed *The Torrents of Spring,* his short satire of Sherwood Anderson's later work. That satiric novella is the antithesis of *The Sun Also Rises;* It glories in authorial comment, outrageous overstatement, and a general lack of effective control. But in it, Hemingway set high standards for Anderson—and for himself. He characterized the task of revising to such high standards this way: "Schruns was a good place to work. I know because I did *the most difficult job of rewriting I have ever done* there in the winter of 1925 and 1926, when I had to take the first draft of *The Sun Also Rises* which I had written in one sprint of six weeks, and make it into a novel" (*MF,* p. 202; my emphasis). In the first draft of the novel, it sometimes seems that Hemingway was conscious that such rewriting would become necessary. At times his comments reflected considerable confusion over where the novel was going and how it should be shaped. He worried over which characters should be at the center of the book; he considered whether or not he was achieving a proper narrative distance from the events of the novel; and he wondered about how his literary friends would receive the work.

Yet at other times he was clearly in control, particularly in control of the overall shape of the book in spite of his concern for the crafting of the novel, which would lead to "the most difficult job of rewriting."

By the time he had written half of the published chapter 10, a little less than a month after he had begun to work on the first draft, Hemingway seemed to be essentially in control of that overall structure. Inside the back cover of his third notebook, Hemingway jotted down an outline projecting that the completed novel would have a total of eighteen chapters. He was being somewhat optimistic in his projection—the notebook draft would eventually comprise twenty-two chapters. But in this outline the major events of the novel's plot line were represented. Included were the involvement of Brett (here called Duff) with Romero (here, Niño de la Palma), Mike's conflicts with Robert Cohn (here, Gerald), and even Jake's eventual return to Spain after Brett's breakup with Romero. The *desencajonada* (the unloading of the bulls), the *encierro* (the driving of the bulls into the pen), and the *corrida* form clear focuses for two for the projected chapters, while Brett's involvement with Romero and the resulting fight between Cohn and Romero will be at the center of another. In its chapter divisions, Hemingway's outline did tend to lump together more material than might fill a chapter in the finished novel. This is part of Hemingway's outline for the novel as it appeared on the back cover of notebook 3:

> Chap XIII—finishes with Gerald not going.
> Chap XIV Ride to Burguete Fishing return to Pamplona.
> Chap XV Duff Gerald and Mike there Desencajonada—which we get in.
> the party out at the wine shop. Mike's first out burst.
> Chap XVI Encierro, first corrida brings back to point where book starts.
> Goes on with that night—the South American. the dancing place.
> Noel Murphy. Count shows up.
> Chap XVII Duff sleeps with Niño de la Palma. Gerald fights with Niño.
> Chap XVIII Corrida. Duff goes off with Niño. Count refuses Mike job.
> Bill goes to Paris. Mike talks, goes to Saint Jean de Luz to wait for
> Duff, Gerald talks, goes to ~~Saint Jean de Luz~~ San Sebastian after-
> wards Paris. I go on down into Spain to bring Duff back. get her
> letter [194-3-53]

Chapter 13 in the notebook draft corresponds to chapter 13 in this outline, ending with Cohn's deciding not to go to Burguete. Since the notebook chapter 14 covers only the ride to Burguete, while the outline projects it as including the entire fishing trip and return to Pamplona, it seems likely that this outline was put together sometime during the writing of notebook chapter 13 or early in the writing of notebook chapter 14.

The trip to Burguete, the fishing, and the trip back to Pamplona eventually filled two and one-half chapters, rather than the single chapter that Hemingway projected in his outline; the section is an idyllic respite from the tensions of the group, and in giving it more space as he wrote, Hemingway provided a more solid base for its juxtaposition to those tensions.* Similarly, the events of the final

---

* It was perhaps in doing so that Hemingway introduced a considerable difficulty—the lack of consistency in dates within the novel. A reader who is concerned with the journalistic

chapter in the outline will make up three chapters in the first draft but only two in the published version of *The Sun Also Rises*. And the events of the short chapter 14 (notebook chap. 17) of *The Sun Also Rises,* in which Jake lies in bed thinking about the group and which then bridges two uneventful days before the beginning of the fiesta, do not correspond to anything listed in the outline. Of course, a good deal of the material of the completed novel cannot be included in so short an outline focusing only on events. However, the correspondence of the outline to the novel's events is fairly exact and can be charted (see table 4.1).

TABLE 4.1

A COMPARISON, BY CHAPTERS, OF THE EVENTS, OUTLINED TO ELEMENTS IN THE FIRST DRAFT AND IN THE PUBLISHED VERSION

Projected Outline	*First Draft*	*"The Sun Also Rises"*
13	13	10
	14	11
14	15	12
	16 (part)	13 (part)
15	16 (part)	13 (part)
No events correspond	17	14
16	18	15
17	19	16
		17
	21*	18
18	21*	19
	22†	

* The two notebook chapters 21 represent a misnumbering. They are separate chapters.
† The chapter 22 heading was apparently written in as the notebook was revised.

Aside from the expansion of the number of chapters in the drafts of the novel, the outline differs in only a few particulars with regard to the characters and events involved in bringing the novel to its close. In the projected description of the party following the first corrida, Hemingway had planned to introduce both a South American (perhaps to work against Robert Cohn's earlier idealization of South

qualities of the novel's first draft will discover that the few dates mentioned within the novel do not match actual dates in 1923, 1924, or 1925 with any consistency. Hemingway tells us the fiesta began on Sunday July 6, which was the case in 1924. However, other 1924 dates do not match. A reader who is less concerned with journalistic accuracy but is interested in an internally accurate if fictional calendar will discover that Hemingway slipped in an extra week or so between the novel's beginning in Paris and the frantic week of the fiesta in Burguete. For a complete timetable see Kermit Vanderbilt's "*The Sun Also Rises:* Time Uncertain," *Twentieth Century Literature* 15 (October 1969): 153–54.

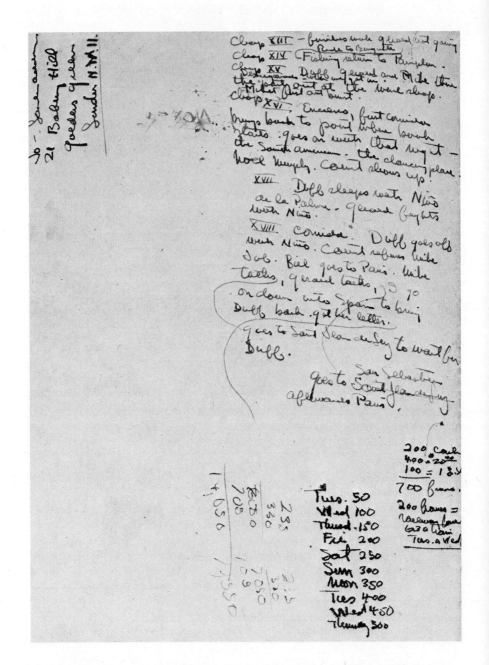

Hemingway's projected outline for chapters 10 on of the published version of *The Sun Also Rises* shares space with jotted accounts and an address (194-3-53).

America) and a character identified only as Noel Murphy (perhaps based on the sister-in-law of Gerald Murphy, the rich expatriate who later contributed much to F. Scott Fitzgerald's characterization of Dick Diver in *Tender Is the Night*). Apparently, Hemingway also planned at the same time to reintroduce Count Mippipopolous, the character out of the novel's Paris section whom many critics have compared to Jake in his knowledge of "the values" for proper living, in his appreciation of the good things of life, and in his bearing of physical wounds as signs of his experience of the world.

According to the outline, in the projected final chapter the count was to have refused to give Mike a job. However, Count Mippipopolous did not reappear at any point as Hemingway finished his first draft or as he revised. While no evidence exists as to exactly why Hemingway chose to ignore this outline and not to reintroduce the count, the choice seems to make sense both dramatically and structurally: the count tends to serve as a calming force whenever he appears, and while the earlier juxtaposition with his character helps the reader to understand Jake, while also illuminating the values that the count exemplifies, his doubling presence in the climax and resolution of the plot might tend to blur our tracking of Jake's reactions and perceptions.

Additionally, the count's presence in the ending of the novel is less necessary than in the Paris section, near the book's beginning, for Jake (and even Brett), the characters who are closely identified with the count, have changed considerably during the course of the novel. The Jake Barnes of the early section, who cries at night over his injury and who finds himself unreasonably jealous when Brett is with other men (particularly Robert Cohn), has learned to accept and live with his limitations. Like the count, he takes pleasure in what is available to him; just as the count comments on Brett and Jake's dancing in Zelli's jazz bar—"I would do it if I would enjoy it"— and says to Brett, "I enjoy to watch you dance" (*SAR,* p. 63), Jake comes to peace. In giving up Romero, Brett has acted more responsibly than we have seen her act before. In the first-draft version of the bar scene, the count is described as "sitting there like Buddah [*sic*]" (194-2), completely serene, though the description is later revised to emphasize the count's serene enjoyment of the pleasures of life: "He was sitting at the table smoking a cigar" (*SAR,* p. 62). By the end of the book, Jake has come closer to the serenity we see exemplified in the count, and the contrast with the count would only have served to emphasize the distance that Jake still had to travel in order to attain full maturity. In the absence of that contrast, we can see how far Jake has come and how he will continue the process of coming to terms with the conditions of his life.

There is another difference between Hemingway's outline and the completed draft. Its significance cannot be precisely established, but it can be explored in a close reading of his outline for the novel's final chapter. Ending the outline, Hemingway writes, "I go on down into Spain to bring Duff back, get her letter" (194-3-53). No letter is received in the ending of the novel, though it is possible that the letter of the outline became, in the first draft, the telegrams calling Jake to

Madrid. However, a strict adherence to chronology, which Hemingway does not otherwise depart from in the outline, would have placed those messages before Jake's trip "down into Spain" rather than after, as the notation appears in the outline. One may conjecture that Hemingway did not plan to have Jake and Brett meet in Madrid, but that Jake might have arrived to find a letter waiting for him. Brett might have left the Hotel Montana before Jake's arrival; even after a meeting, she might have written to him to explain her feelings and actions. If either were the case, Hemingway obviously chose in the first draft to work through a meeting of the two. And the meeting of Jake and Brett, which leads to their bittersweet meal and the final taxi ride together, accomplishes the novel's resolution at once more movingly and more economically than any letter or exchange of letters could have done. In the events of the meeting and in the talks between the two, we see Jake and Brett as closely as possible, at firsthand. Their language is more naturally expressive and their actions are more revealing than the language of a letter could have been.

Hemingway later rejected another use of a letter—the letter that Bill mentions having received from the black boxer he befriended in Vienna. Apparently Hemingway had trouble deciding what the boxer would write: in the notebook draft, Hemingway left enough space for the letter to be written in—blank space equaling a notebook page is headed "Köln/Dear Mr. Grundy" and ends with "yours fondly/William Tate." After reading the letter, Jake comments, "That's a letter," and Bill echoes, "You're darn right that's a letter" (194-2-41 and 42). But Hemingway never filled in the blank space as he revised: there is no evidence that he ever wrote anything to fill it.

Instead, in the second draft, Hemingway substituted new material after the first-draft description of what had happened in Vienna, as told to Jake by the half-drunk Bill Gorton. Bill's description of the fixed fight and its aftermath is splendidly comic; Hemingway continued the comic tone in Bill's delightfully fractured discussion of values as they relate to stuffed animals. ("Simple exchange of values. You give them money. They give you a stuffed dog. . . . Road to hell paved with unbought stuffed dogs" [*SAR*, pp. 72-73].)

Long-distance communication always tends to be inadequate in *The Sun Also Rises*. Bill's tale offers a more direct impression of the events in Vienna than the deleted letter could have, and the tone of his discussion about stuffed dogs tells much more about his essential gentleness and his accurate perception of the world than the boxer's written expression of gratitude could have conveyed. The meeting between Jake and Brett in Madrid is also more evocative than an exchange of letters could have been—in the published book, the contrast between Brett's terse telegram, "COULD YOU COME HOTEL MONTANA MADRID AM RATHER IN TROUBLE" (*SAR*, p.238), and her conversation with Jake is extraordinary.

Similarly, Robert's earlier telegram to Jake tells next to nothing: "Vengo Jueves Cohn" (*SAR*, p. 127). Cohn is justifiably ridiculed by Bill and Jake for failing to use the ten words that he could have sent for the same price as his

A blank in the first draft, intended for the letter that Hemingway left space for but never completed, instead substituting a more direct presentation through Bill Gorton (194-2-41 and 42) pompous-sounding message "I come Thursday." Even Bill is less than completely expressive in his post card to Jake, here quoted in full: "Jake, Budapest is wonderful" (*SAR*, p. 70). Surprisingly, the best communication is the letter from Mike explaining why he and Brett will be late arriving in Pamplona. While the letter is marred by an overuse of the conventional "all our love," it also contains one of Mike's clearest statements of his love for Brett: "I know her so well and try to look after her but it's not so easy" *SAR*, p. 126).

The cables that Jake writes in his Paris office are professional rather than personal communications, and all the other telegrams that appear in the novel are concerned only with physical comings and goings. The meanings of all such messages seem as cryptic as Brett's "AM RATHER IN TROUBLE." At most, they only hint at the needs and emotions felt by their senders. In *The Sun Also Rises*, real communication can take place only face-to-face, perhaps even with the ritual touch on the shoulder that marks the recognition of one aficionado by another.

In his rejection of the use of letters and telegrams to carry important communications between characters, as well as in his refusal to use them as narrative devices to convey information that is important to the reader, Hemingway chose an immediate, direct narration. As he again and again demonstrated the banality of long-distance communication, Hemingway underlined his choice of an immediate and involved first-person narration, what Sheldon Norman Grebstein, in *Hemingway's Craft*, called a point of view that "evolves out of a sense of the continuous present, of the narrator's close proximity in time to the events he recounts" (p. 72).

The evidence indicates that in the shaping of his narrative method, Hemingway was not without his doubts as to Jake Barnes's ability to do an adequate job of presenting the story. Again and again in the first draft, Jake muses on the efficacy of his narration. The critics have also addressed the question, with varying results. A good deal of criticism has focused on Jake's reliability as narrator, particularly on his ability to present Robert Cohn clearly; and evaluations of the novel have occasionally gone so far as to view Cohn as the best character in the book, the optimistic alternative to the sad reality of Jake and Brett's many failures, as does William L. Vance in his "Implications of Form in *The Sun Also Rises*."

Certainly, Jake is not always to be trusted when he begins to analyze other characters: for example, he has reason enough not to view Cohn with an unjaundiced eye, given that both men are hopelessly in love with Brett. Yet, in "the continuous present," Jake faithfully reports all that is going on in Paris and at the fiesta. And he is not unaware of his own biases.

Again and again in the notebook draft the narrator considers his own reliability and the developing shape of the novel. (If in these analytic passages the writer should be thought of as Jake or as Hemingway may be open to question.) Several of these passages found their way into the completed *The Sun Also Rises*, as, for example, in chapter 6, where Jake muses, "Somehow I feel I have not shown Robert Cohn clearly" (*SAR*, p. 45). In this case the comment, which has a potential bearing on narrative method and reliability, leads into a discussion of Cohn's character, in particular his incapacity for distinguishing himself. Of Cohn's optimistic cheerfulness, Jake comments, "I probably have not brought it out" (*SAR,* p. 45). Again, the potential opening for a discussion of method is suppressed. Rather than following with an exposition of his own biases, Jake continues with a discussion of Cohn's youthful love of tennis. Even in the first draft, this section exists essentially as it was published, skirting about a discussion of method, but leading instead through the admission of potential narrative unreliability to a discussion of character. The potential unreliability is brought to the attention of the reader, but it is not resolved.

Yet in the composition of *The Sun Also Rises,* discussion of narrative difficulties—matters of structure, characterization, and emphasis—formed an integral part of Hemingway's method. Thus, at the end of the notebook draft version of *The Sun Also Rises,* chapter 5, just after his argument with Cohn over Duff, the narrator considers the problems of character emphasis that are inherent in the book-length work: "Now you can see. I looked as though I were trying to get to be the hero of this story. But that was all wrong. Gerald Cohn is the hero. When I bring myself in it is only to clear up something. Or maybe Duff is the hero. Or Nino de la Palma. But He never really had a chance to be the hero. Or maybe there is not any hero at all. Maybe a story is better without any hero" (194-2-7). Like a number of similar remarks, this passage was crossed out in Hemingway's revision of the notebooks. It never appeared in any of the typed drafts of the novel. It remains partly significant in its suggestion that Hemingway's story was shifting on him, refusing to follow exactly the lines he may have set out for it. That is, rather than finding that he was writing a wholly predictable work, Hemingway seems to have been discovering that even within his projected structure, the exact shape of the novel was not wholly predictable.

The statement is perhaps even more significant as it leads to its concluding sentence: "Maybe a story is better without any hero." This statement originally stood in a position of extreme emphasis, at the end of the chapter. What Hemingway has suggested is, of course, that maybe a story is better if it moves away from conventional expectations of what elements it should contain. Just as Hemingway projected a fiction without any of the conventional literary signs to the plot's significant moments, he also worked toward a fiction that acknowledged the ambiguities and paradoxes in the personalities of real people. A clear and admirable hero is the backbone of formulaic fiction; a hero (like Cohn) who is far from strong and admirable exists at a remove from such a conventional hero. But in having a possibly confusing multiplicity of heroes or even in not having any character who can be called a hero, Hemingway reaffirmed his movement away from a conventional fiction toward a fiction founded on the careful examination and re-creation of life.

Of course, this emphasis was not newly formed in *The Sun Also Rises*. While such very early evidence as the typescripts of "The Woppian Way," alternatively

Hemingway worked out a question of character emphasis and value in the first draft of his novel. The discussion of ''the hero'' was crossed out at an early stage in the revision (194-2-7).

titled "The Passing of Pickles McCarty"—an unpublished short story that Hemingway wrote in Petoskey, Michigan, and intended for *Argosy*—indicates that he started with formulaic fiction, he soon moved away from such writing. In *A Moveable Feast,* he remembered his faith in the methods that he chose to employ despite the disappointment of repeatedly sending out stories he had faith in and repeatedly having the manuscripts come back (pp. 73–75). His reaction to and movement away from the conventional story was clearly fixed in the writing of the stories and of the chapters of *In Our Time.* Passages such as the one quoted above indicate his reconsideration and reaffirmation of his own directions in the new form, the novel.

These discussions of method and direction in the first draft also seemed to serve as Hemingway's notes to himself, clarifying in an expository manner ideas that he later treated more organically within the scenes of the novel. Thus, at the point where Hemingway wrote that Niño de la Palma "never really had a chance to be the hero" (194-2-7), we have really only seen Niño in the first scene of the first draft, in his hotel room. As the plot returned to Niño later in the notebook draft and as, in later drafts, Hemingway collected the material referring to Niño at the center of the novel's chronology of action, he indeed had a chance to be the hero. Or, more accurately, he contributed, in the character of Pedro Romero, to Hemingway's controlling vision of what sorts of action might make a person admirable, or "heroic."

While we might identify Jake Barnes as the narrator-protagonist, Jake cannot eventually be identified as *the* hero of the novel, even though he looks as if he "were trying to get to be the hero of this story" (194-2-7). Hemingway does not seem to have been using the term *hero* as a technical synonym for *protagonist.* His idea of the hero is separated by the word's innumerable connotations from the far less complicated word *protagonist,* and *The Sun Also Rises* finally offers no hero, but instead a composite vision and presentation of the heroic (and unheroic) as it operates in the world.

Hemingway had examined heroism in his early stories. Aside from his high-school writings, which tend somewhat to overblown supernaturalism, and very early stories that he probably did not have in Paris with him, only three stories seem to have survived from the batch of manuscripts of stories and a novel that was stolen from Hadley Hemingway on the train to Lausanne in December of 1922. One was the sexually explicit "Up in Michigan," which Gertrude Stein judged *inaccrochable,* good but unpublishable. In the other two, "The Woppian Way" and "My Old Man," Hemingway tried to create heroic protagonists. The hero of "The Woppian Way," Pickles McCarty, is a pure, formula-fiction hero. A ranked boxer who has a shot at the championship, he chooses to give up fame in the ring in order to fight as a member of the Arditi, the shock troops on the Italian Front. This 1919 story is less than successful as serious fiction, though it is often sidesplittingly funny—both by intention and by chance—and its too-heroic hero explains that he could never feel the same thrill in the ring after the real fighting in Italy.

In "My Old Man," begun in 1919 and often identified as being derivative of Sherwood Anderson's race-track stories, Hemingway examined heroism from a far-more-insightful standpoint. The Old Man of the title is a jockey, who is seen as nearly heroic by the story's narrator, the jockey's young son. And the story revolves around the son's discovery, after his father's death, that he had been seeing only a part of his father's character. While seemingly an ideal and beloved parent, the father had also been a crooked jockey. After the boy discovers his father's flaws, a friend reassures him that his father was "one swell guy." But the son is not convinced: "Seems like when they get started they don't leave a guy nothing" (*IOT*, p. 173). As readers, we can see what the son cannot immediately comprehend in his disappointment and grief—namely, that the father is simultaneously admirable and terribly flawed: he is human.

The Sun Also Rises presents a composite of such all-too-human characters, each contributing to Hemingway's vision of what is most admirable and courageous in human action in a flawed and dangerous world. In spite of his sometime lack of maturity and his prejudice, Jake Barnes partially represents the hero in his attempts to live honorably in the face of his physical and emotional handicaps. Niño/Romero, in spite of his youth, perhaps comes closest to being an idealized hero in his explorations of frontiers of bravery and artistry. Duff/Brett is a female hero as she finally faces her limitations and accepts responsibility for the damage that she might cause if she follows her own desires. Even Robert Cohn represents a portion of the heroic vision in his loyalty and idealism, however misplaced those qualities may seem, particularly as seen through Jake's less-than-wholly-objective eyes.

Hemingway again and again touched on the idea of lack of control, of a story taking its own directions and imposing its own organic imperatives on the telling of it. In a discussion that first appeared in the notebook draft and survived into the galley proofs before being cut—the passage would have started the second chapter of the beginning that he canceled at the galley stage—Hemingway discussed, through Jake, the problem of distancing the narrator from his narration:

> I did not want to tell this story in the first person but I find that I must. I wanted to stay well outside of the story so that I would not be touched by it in any way, and handle all the people in it with that irony and pity that are so essential to good writing. I even thought I might be amused by all the things that are going to happen to Lady Brett Ashley and Mr. Robert Cohn and Michael Campbell, Esq., and Mr. Jake Barnes. But I made the unfortunate mistake, for a writer, of first having been Mr. Jake Barnes. So it is not going to be splendid and cool and detached after all. "What a pity!" as Brett used to say. [This version is from 202a, galley 2, one of the omitted galley proofs.]

Two possible immediate literary sources have been discovered for Jake's espousal of Anatole France's principles of "irony and pity" as touchstones for good writing. Perhaps the more likely of the two was Gilbert Seldes's 1925 review in the *Dial* of another 1920s classic-to-be: *The Great Gatsby.* In the review, Seldes praised Fitzgerald effusively; in *A Moveable Feast,* Hemingway acknowledged that he had been shown the review by Fitzgerald, noting that the review "could only have been better if Gilbert Seldes had been better" (*MF,* p. 154). Seldes said that Fitzgerald had "ceased to content himself with a satiric report on the outside of American life and has with considerable irony attacked the spirit underneath" and that Fitzgerald was "regarding a tiny section of life and reporting it with irony and pity and a consuming passion" (pp. 163, 162). The review also ranks Ftizgerald as having far surpassed all the men of his generation. A second possible source for the phrase was the title of a collection of stories published early in 1926 by the American author Paul Eldridge: *Irony and Pity: A Book of Tales.* However, the second draft of *The Sun Also Rises* had been completed by the end of March 1926, and the first review of Eldridge's book did not appear until late in March 1926, though Hemingway might have seen the collection of stories during his February 1926 trip to New York. Either of these two sources, of course, might also have helped to recall Don Stewart's comment on the irony and pity of the ruin of the Irati River.*

As Hemingway discussed the difficulties of first-person narration, he suggested his desire to achieve an appropriate narrative distance while at the same time poking fun at the conventional "splendid and cool and detached" stance. The references to the intrusive necessity of the first-person narration not only serve dramatically to characterize Jake as a person drawn in, against his judgment and will, to emotional involvement in the story that he narrates, but also suggest Hemingway's acute consciousness of the form in which he was working. Most of his fiction to this point had allowed him the splendid, cool, and detached stance of the third-person narrator, excepting only "My Old Man," five of the chapters of *In Our Time* (1, 3, 4, 13, and "L'Envoi"), and the still unpublished "The Woppian Way." But none of the first-person narrators in these pieces of fiction, with the possible exception of the interviewer of "L'Envoi," is particularly a consciously perceiving character. In the chapters, Hemingway was trying different personae—a kitchen corporal, a British officer, a matador—as he tried out the persona of the young boy in "My Old Man" and that of the cynical middle-aged newspaperman who narrates "The Woppian Way." Particularly in the chapters, he was presenting character through speech, rather than exploring the use of a central consciousness as a narrative screen or focus for the presentation of a story. Joe Butler, the disillusioned boy narrator of "My Old Man," comes closest to working as such a central screen, yet Joe does not have the maturity, the tendency toward introspection, and the lack of involvement, which might qualify a narrator to view with irony and pity the events and characters that he portrays.

If Hemingway indeed felt challenged to reproduce Fitzgerald's achievement in *The Great Gatsby,* working though an involved yet peripheral narrator like Nick

---

* Scott Donaldson traces the sources in " 'Irony and Pity'—Anatole France Got It Up," in *Fitzgerald/Hemingway Annual* (Detroit: Gale Research Co., 1978), pp. 331–34.

Carraway, his earlier work had not completely prepared him for such a form of narration. And as he wrote, he discovered a different narration arising out of the events and characters of the novel. His narrator had seen and experienced far more than a Nick Carraway, had made "the unfortunate mistake, for a writer, of first having been Mr. Jake Barnes" (202a, galley 2). And Jake is far closer to the center of the novel that he narrates than Nick is to the center of *The Great Gatsby*. The narrative scheme of *The Sun Also Rises* was not to be "so splendid and cool and detached," but Hemingway would take up another challenge posed by Seldes's review of *Gatsby*, a review that he would remember even thirty-odd years later as he wrote *A Moveable Feast*—namely, to recognize, as Fitzgerald did, "both his capacities and his obligations as a novelist" and to match Fitzgerald's "extraordinary . . . technical virtuosity" (Seldes, pp. 164, 162).

Of irony, *The Sun Also Rises* contains a great deal, beginning with the terrible irony of Jake's injury and continuing through all of the effects that the injury had on his perceptions of the world around him; but of pity there seems to be very little. Pity is precisely the emotion that Jake must carefully guard against, lest self-pity overwhelm him and lest the terrible irony of his situation degenerate into mere banality, as nearly happens in Jake's dinner conversation with Georgette, when they discuss the wound and the war. Jake recognizes the danger: "We would probably have gone on and discussed the war and agreed that it was in reality a calamity for civilization, and perhaps would have been better avoided. I was bored enough" (*SAR*, p. 17). And Hemingway must similarly guard against the expression of the emotion in his narrative scheme, since he has committed himself to an art which creates rather than discusses reality.

As he revised, Hemingway reduced the novel's discussions of irony and pity, removing Jake's discussion of "that irony and pity that are so essential to good writing" and also deleting another discussion that centered on Brett's "What a pity!" The remaining reference to the concepts comes in the context of Jake and Bill's idyllic fishing trip to Burguete, as Bill begins the morning by singing, "Irony and Pity. When you're feeling . . . [shitty]. Oh, Give them Irony and Give them Pity" (*SAR*, p. 114). The passage probably should be read as a sly dig at Fitzgerald. Or perhaps Bill is making an even more obscure reference to the recent publication of *Irony and Pity*, a book of short stories by Paul Eldridge, since Bill had just arrived with the latest news from literary New York. But while Bill's mocking treatment undercuts the seriousness of irony and pity as principles guiding action or literary composition, Hemingway subtly—and ironically—underlines their significance to Jake in one of the relatively few handwritten additions to his own typescript second draft of the second half of the novel. He lines in the title of the tune that Bill is singing: "The Bells are Ringing for Me and My Gal" (198-1-35)— but not for Jake Barnes and his gal. The point is made succinctly, without direct comment from either Jake, the narrator, or Hemingway, the author. But the irony is perhaps too neat; he later took the song title back out.

Hemingway seems to have been ever aware of the dangers of overstatement, but his method of composition in the first draft worked from overstatement and

In the first draft, Hemingway discussed his method, ''these special moments that novelists build their whole structures on,'' and his literary friends' expectations of him (194-1-9).

direct comment to the reader. Early in the first notebook, just after having commented that "none of the significant things are going to have any literary signs marking them," he went on to comment on his own comments:

> Now when my friends read this they will say it is awful; ~~it is not what they had hoped or expected from me.~~ Gertrude Stein once told me that remarks are not literature. All right, let it go at that. Only this time all the remarks are going in and if it is not literature who claimed it was anyway. [194-1-9]

And the "remarks" did go into the first draft; they helped Hemingway to clarify directions and to solidify ideas as he hammered out his first draft in five different cities over a period of two months. Perhaps, like the passage quoted above, they also helped to discharge some of the tension of writing for an audience that very definitely hoped for and expected great things from him, an audience of recognized writers who had their own ideas of what made "literature." Eventually, all the "remarks" that found their way into the first draft of the novel disappeared as Hemingway revised.

As Hemingway moved through the first draft of the novel, his manuscript reflected more and more overt consideration of the implications of the elements that shape *The Sun Also Rises*. He explored the linkings and oppositions among elements of his narration. The novel's assemblage of elements may seem random to the casual reader (American novelist Nathan Asch read part of the manuscript and then told Hemingway that he was writing a "travel book" rather than a novel), but Hemingway carefully considered each part's relationship to the whole, and *The Sun Also Rises* is actually tightly reasoned and tightly structured.

In part, the novel is a "travel book," but it is first a novel whose settings have received particular attention. Early in the first notebook of the first draft, the narrator reflects on whether to include extensive descriptions of the expatriates' life in Paris's Montmartre quarter, descriptions that make up a good deal of Book I of *The Sun Also Rises*. The tone of his consideration is similar to that of a 25 March 1922 feature article, "American Bohemians in Paris," published by Hemingway in the *Toronto Star Weekly*. In that early article he reflected that Montmartre's bars were filled nightly with expatriates—but not by serious artists and writers. The inmates of bars like the Rotonde "are nearly all loafers expending the energy that an artist puts into his creative work in talking about what they are going to do" (*Byline*, p. 25).

Within the draft of his novel, Hemingway again considered the quarter, but he began from a more personalized perspective than in the *Toronto Star Weekly* article, first discussing Pat and Duff (later to be Mike and Brett) as drunks and then going on to explain the importance of his descriptions to the meaning of his story and particularly the relevance of the quarter to two of the novel's potential "heroes," Romero and Cohn. Just after the description of Pat and Duff came this remark: "I ~~don't~~ not know why I have put all this down. It may mix up the story but I wanted to show you what a fine crowd we were; what a good crowd for a nineteen year old kid [Romero] to get in with'' (194-1-6 and 7). Some ten or twelve notebook pages later, Hemingway concludes his extensive description of expatriate life in Paris with these seemingly paradoxical yet significant statements: The quarter "is too sad and dull a place to write about. I have to put it in because Gerald [Cohn] had spent two years in it. That accounts for a great many things" (194-1-12).

The morally dissolute life of Paris accounted, indeed, for a great deal of what was to follow. And the character-to-character tensions set up in the quarter are eventually released in the frenzy of another setting, Pamplona at fiesta time. Just as Hemingway analyzed the role of the Paris setting in shaping the events of the novel, later in the first draft he considered the Pamplona fiesta—but with a very different conclusion, that the fiesta's role was not causative, but catalytic:

> I do not think English and Americans have ever had any seven day fiestas. A prolonged fiesta does strange things to them. Pamplona is a reckless fiesta and *it can be dangerous. It can be just* a dangerous fiesta. Whether the danger grew up out of the recklessness or the recklessness out of the danger I do not know.
>
> How much of what happened can be laid to the fiesta and how much must be laid to the natural progress of events starting in Paris I cannot decide. The fiesta made every one a little crazy certainly but it had the effect of speeding up the natural tendencies through this insistence on the unimportance of consequences. Still I think it is only incidental to the story. If it had not been the Fiesta it would have been something else.
>
> It was a fiesta and it went on for seven days. [194-5-2; the italicized section was added in revision. This would have followed the first sentence on p. 155 of *SAR*.]

Here again, Hemingway quite consciously was working out the structure of the novel on paper. In this passage he began by seeming to be unsure of the exact role of the fiesta in influencing the actions of his characters, and he ended with absolute certainty, moving from the early "I do not know," through the statement of possible forms for the relationship of action to setting ("I cannot decide"), to the eventual decision "If it had not been the Fiesta it would have been something else."

Just a few pages after the beginning of the published chapter 15, as "the fiesta exploded," he has decided upon the essentially catalytic rather than causative role of the celebration. "The unimportance of consequences" was not directly presented in the final draft, but was represented in the lines of chapter 15's first paragraph, where Jake comments that to the peasants early in the fiesta, "money still had a definite value in hours worked and bushels of grain sold. Late in the fiesta it would not matter what they paid, nor where they bought" (*SAR*, p. 152). Hemingway's *consideration* has been replaced by Jake's *presentation*.

Late in the first draft, as Jake recuperates in San Sebastián before Brett's telegrams reach him, functional elements of setting are again considered; later in the writing of the novel these considerations have been deleted and the effect of place upon Jake has been shown rather than analyzed. Again and again in what became the published chapter 19, one of the most heavily revised sections of the novel, we find such statements as this: "It was a splendid place to swim. You could lie on the beach and soak in the sun and get straightened around inside again. Maybe I would feel like writing. San Sebastian was a good place" (196-6-31; corresponds to *SAR*, p. 232). Or, again a few pages later, Jake continues his consideration of the differences between France and Spain, as he has lunch: "It was pleasant to have too much a great amount of food served again. You did not have to eat it and it was nice not to have that measured French feeling" (194-6-34; corresponds to *SAR*, p. 234). And yet again a few pages later: "San Sebastian was a good place. It was a good place to get all straightened inside again. . . . Then I could go back to Paris and get to work again" (194-6-36; corresponds to *SAR*, p. 235).

By this point in the composition process, however, the exact function of these considerations of place seems to have altered somewhat as Hemingway gained a surer sense of his method. The speaking voice has changed: in notebook one, when Hemingway wrote that "all the remarks are going in," the speaking voice was clearly that of Ernest Hemingway, author; in the consideration of the Pamplona fiesta and the telling of the story in the first person, the speaker is more ambiguously identified, at once representing a convergence of the actual and implied authors' interests. In the near-obsessive concern with getting straightened around inside, the considerations of San Sebastián clearly operate to characterize Jake Barnes's mental state; these and other of Jake's statements near the end of the first draft seem to project a protagonist who is more bitter and less in control of himself than the Jake Barnes of the completed novel, and a Jake Barnes who is not at all transcribed out of Hemingway's own experiences at Pamplona but has been completely transformed, completely created as an independent character.

While Jake developed early and naturally as narrator, Hemingway seemed to have had a few second thoughts as to his effectiveness; Jake's desire to avoid writing the story in the first person was at least in part the reflection of a desire on Hemingway's part. In his revisions of the novel, Hemingway considered a third-person beginning, even going as far as to type out two fragmentary versions of the first draft that began in Romero's hotel room. In the second version, the narrator was not only in the third person but was also omniscient. These two trials were far from satisfactory, however; they seem lifeless beside Jake's narration, and Hemingway soon abandoned them. The longer of the two trials covered only five typewritten pages.

Hemingway's impulse toward a third-person narration did not bear fruit; nevertheless, in the course of composing the first draft and in subsequent revision, he did introduce a narrative perspective, which was markedly different from that of Jake, in the person of Bill Grundy (who was later renamed Bill Gorton). Effectively, Bill is a second—though secondary—narrator. Within Jake's narration, Bill is a storyteller, recounting, for example, the adventures he undertook in

we played three handed bridge
with an Englishman who had
walked over from Sainte-Jean-Pied-
de-Port for the fishing and stopped
at the inn for the fishing. He
was very pleasant and went
with us twice to the Irati River.
There was no word from Duff
and no word from Mike.

Chapter ~~XVI~~

One morning I went down
to breakfast and the Englishman
was already at the table. He was
reading the paper through spectacles.
He looked up and grinned.
"Good morning," he said.
"Settin' for you... I stopped at
the post and they gave it me
with mine."
I was at my place at the

table, leaning against a coffee
cup. The Englishman, his name was
Harris, was looking... receiving the
paper again. I opened the
letter. It had been forwarded from
Pamplona. I was dated San
Sebastian; Sunday.

Dear Jake..

We got here Friday and so
brought her here for three days rest
with our friend Braddocks. We go to
Quintana Hotel Pamplona Thursday.
... don't know exactly when... Will
you send a note by
the bus to tell us what to do to
rejoin you... on Wednesday and
be late, but
Duff was really close in and will
be quite all right by Tues and is
practically so now. I know her so
well and try to look after
her but its not so easy. So take care

The marginal note indicates a possible experiment in using the character of Bill Gorton as an alternative narrator. Notice the crossed-out notes beside the chapter heading (194-4-16).

befriending the black boxer in Vienna. Later, Bill will serve as a second controlling consciousness in Hemingway's presentation of the fiesta. Jake's point of view is expanded and enriched as Bill recounts events of the chaotic celebration that he, rather than Jake, has witnessed firsthand. (Mike Campbell similarly serves to expand Jake's viewpoint, as he tells, at Bill's urging, about Cohn's fight with Romero.)

And for several pages in the Burguete section of the first draft, Bill becomes the novel's narrator. At the beginning of chapter 16 of that draft, the identity of the speaker seems to be confused. Where the published version reads *I,* the notebook draft reads *Jake;* and where the published version reads *Bill,* the notebook reads *I.* Bill is telling the story directly to the reader. A note in the margin of the notebook reads: "1st person now Bill—Friend now" (194-4-16). Later in the process of composition (perhaps when Hemingway reworked the novel in Schruns, though no definite proof exists for this tentative dating beyond Hemingway's general statement about the revision of the novel) another marginal note was added beneath the first: "change to Jake/be [nearly illegible, probably *tragic*] throughout" (194-4-16). Eventually, both notations were very heavily crossed out, and the identifications of the speakers were reversed to fit in with a continuation of Jake's point of view. It will never be possible to know whether Hemingway intended only to attempt to write one chapter from Bill's point of view or whether he was considering some sort of alternating structure, using Bill and Jake as complementary comic and "tragic" filters through which to view the events that were taking place in Spain. While Bill might have added a comic or ironic perspective (as, indeed, he does in the final version of *The Sun Also Rises*), his inclusion as a second narrator would have considerably compromised the unity of the novel's narrative scheme. In any case. Hemingway continued the experiment for only a few pages before abandoning it.

In revision, however, Bill was developed as a storyteller; the "stuffed dog" section, for example, which runs from near the top of page 72 to the appearance of Brett on page 74, was a late addition, first appearing in the typist's version of the second draft.

5
"The Most Difficult Job of Revision"

While in most cases the typescript second draft of *The Sun Also Rises* corresponds closely to the published book and while even many sections of the earlier notebook draft match the final novel closely, in a number of instances Hemingway's continued revision of certain scenes can be traced through a number of drafts. In terms of an understanding of his methods and principles, several such scenes can serve as instructive examples, particularly when they represent the presentations of material that is important to the development of theme or character in the novel. I have chosen to discuss four such scenes. They are (1) the early love scene between Jake and Brett, which appears in the published version in chapter 7; (2) the discussion by Jake and a waiter of the death of Vicente Girones, the peasant who is gored while running before the bulls; (3) the description of Romero's performance in the bullring before Jake and Brett on the day after he has been beaten by Robert Cohn; and (4) the final chapter of the book, in which Jake leaves his friends and then returns to take Brett out of Spain.

In each of these four scenes, Hemingway was working with material which had not proved to be satisfactory in its first-draft form, working to handle such material in a manner that would properly integrate it into the action and the tone of the entire novel. And in each of these sections to be examined, he was working farthest from that clear, lyrical gift of first-draft composition that often operated in his work and that resulted in a first draft that was essentially identical to the version of a scene that he eventually selected for publication. (In *A Moveable Feast* Hemingway called this phenomenon the story "writing itself," or flowing out onto the page [*MF*, p. 6].) To use his own term, in the four scenes to be discussed, the book was no longer "writing itself"; here Hemingway was being forced to write it.

Hemingway in Schruns, Austria, during the winter of 1925/26, the winter of the "most difficult job of revision" (photo. no. EH 7284N, John F. Kennedy Library)

That is, his solutions to problems in composition were not immediate and intuitive, as was sometimes the case elsewhere, but rather were a matter of carefully working toward an appropriate effect.

Each scene posed a somewhat different problem for Hemingway. In the love scene between Brett and Jake, the essential difficulty was one of delicacy and restraint; the solution, arrived at through many drafts, followed the iceberg principle. The conversation between the two lovers was ruthlessly pared down to an irreducible minimum, which suggests the terrible restraints that govern the relationship while avoiding a tendency toward the overly sentimental dialogue that intruded in the early draft.

In the discussion of the death of Vicente Girones, Hemingway faced again a problem of delicacy in presentation as well as the necessity of providing, in a few pages, an alternative and condemnatory view on the value of the corrida. Here the essential length and shape of the conversation between Jake and the waiter did *not* change from draft to draft—exactly the opposite of what happened in the revision of the love scene. Rather, Hemingway solved his difficulties by sensitively revising line by line, by searching for *le mot juste*. While he made some deletions, he did not cross out entire segments of the conversation, as in the Jake/Brett scene, but deleted a word or two here or changed at most a phrase there.

In the corrida scene, Hemingway faced a problem of exemplification—the scene lets us as readers see through the eyes of the narrator that Romero's spirit and worth remain unblemished, however much Robert Cohn has marked Romero physically. Here Hemingway operated partially on the principle of the iceberg, removing elements (mostly Jake's comments and his comparisons of Romero to other bullfighters) in order to ensure that his readers would focus on the central, immediately occurring action. But even more, Hemingway operated in this revision by making substitutions. While the essential framework of the action, the killing of two bulls, remained the same, he made great changes within that framework, deleting early-draft descriptions of Romero's actions and substituting later material, which was completely different and which much more adequately exemplified Romero's character through action.

The final chapter is one of the sections of the novel that was most extensively revised within the framework established for it in the first draft. Here again Hemingway worked by deleting large blocks of narrative explanation, as well as by intensively revising in search of *le mot juste*. He also made substitutions, replacing direct and unrestrained narrative statements by indirect presentations of far greater subtlety.

In this final chapter, of course, Hemingway's difficulties were compounded, for the chapter must work effectively as an immediate experience while also serving to tie together and resolve the multiple strands of mood, characterization, action, and theme that have wound their way through the entire novel. The importance of this final chapter was underlined by Hemingway's eventual designation of it as Book III of the complete work, by implication a section that was equal in weight and importance to the seven-chapter Book I, which introduces the Paris-Montmartre background, and the ten-chapter Book II, which constitutes the main action (in Paris, Burguete, and Pamplona) of the novel.

THE FIRST SCENE: JAKE AND BRETT ALONE

Early in the novel, around page 55, Brett and Jake sit together on Jake's bed. It is evening; Brett has just sent her escort, Count Mippipopolous, out for champagne so that she and Jake can talk.

Hemingway expended considerable effort on revising this scene, particularly on the section in which Jake and Brett most directly discuss their love for each other. In the published version, the essence of the conversation is contained in this exchange between the two, with Brett maintaining her distance as a defense against the pain inherent in the impossibility of the whole relationship, given Jake's wound:

> "Isn't it rotten? There isn't any use my telling you I love you."
> "You know I love you." [says Jake]
> "Let's not talk. Talking's all bilge. I'm going away from you, and then Michael's coming back." [*SAR*, p. 55]

Words are inadequate to the situation, and Brett's rejection of them at once serves to characterize her, to define the situation, and to introduce a thematic distrust of verbal communication which is later most clearly shown as the aficionados of the corrida must *touch* Jake before they are willing to believe him as fellow aficionado. For Jake and Brett, of course, touching is impossible, and words are inadequate to express the lovers' feelings; but in earlier versions, words were even less adequate, neither meaningful nor seemly. The lovers became maudlin— words ran away with and overwhelmed the exchange. The notebook first-draft version of the conversation was much longer:

> "Isn[']t it rotten.[?] You know I feel rather quiet and ~~good~~ cool today ~~too~~. It's good to talk it out now when we're quiet. *[There]* I *[i]sn't any use my telling you I love you.*"
> *"You know I love you."*
> "I love you and I'll love you always ~~and~~. I never told any man that."
> "I love you and I'll love you always."
> "It's terrible loving when you've loved so many times that you know what it is."
> "I don't know. I've never loved a lot of people."
> "Yes you have."
> "Not the same way."
> "Oh l*[L]et[']s not talk. Talking's all bilge. I'm going away from you [,] and then* ~~Mike's~~ *Michael's coming back.*" [194-2-28; italics indicate the elements that Hemingway eventually chose to include in the published work; square brackets indicate changes that he made.]

The eventual reduction from 109 words, constituting 9 units of dialogue, to 34 words, constituting 4 units, heightens the desperation of the situation as well as the ironic commentary upon the different meanings of the word *love*. In this first-draft version the tension of the situation is obscured by a torrent of words; indeed, Brett's statement on talking it out "now when we're quiet" operates in opposition to the thematic distrust of words and in opposition to Brett's essential wary toughness. And here the repetition of "I love you" carries no weight. It merely seems trite—it is not the sort of repetition that Gertrude Stein termed *insistence,* the haunting periodic repetition of a word or phrase that so often marks Hemingway's best work.

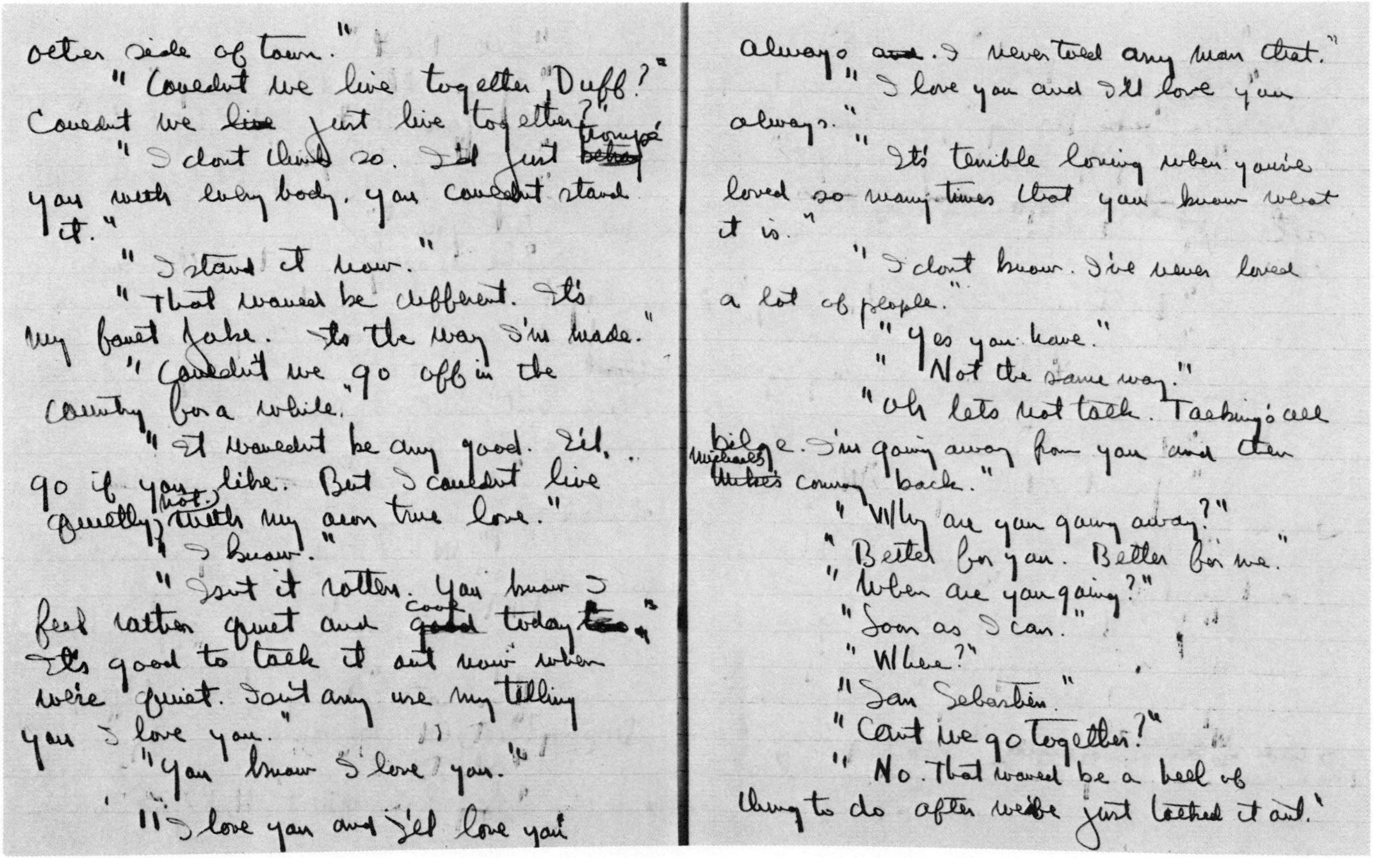

[Handwritten manuscript facsimile]

other side of town."

"Couldn't we live together Duff?"
Couldn't we just live together?"

"I don't think so. I'd just ... you with everybody. You couldn't stand it."

"I stand it now."

"That would be different. It's my fault ... the way I'm made."

"Couldn't we go off in the country for a while."

"It wouldn't be any good. ... I'd ... live. But I couldn't live quietly with my own true love."

"I know."

"Isn't it rotten. ... you know I ... feel rather ... and ... today ..."

"It's good to talk ... and ... we're quiet. Isn't any use my telling you ... love you."

"You know I love you."

"I love you and I'll love you

always. I never told any man that."

"I love you and I'll love you always."

"It's terrible loving when you're loved so many times that you know what it is."

"I don't know. She never loved a lot of people."

"Yes you have."

"Not the same way."

"Oh let's not talk. Talking; all ... ... going away from you. And then ..."

"Why are you going away?"

"Better for you. Better for me."

"When are you going?"

"Soon as I can."

"Where?"

"San Sebastian."

"Can't we go together?"

"No. That would be a hell of ... would just ... it after."

The original version of Jake and Brett's avowal of love for each other. In revising, Hemingway pared away the excess of words, thus achieving a far more impressive effect (194-2-28).

true love. *If I'd ever had one —* "

"I know."

"Isn't it rotten ? Isn't any use my telling
you I love you."

"You know I love you."

"I love you and I'll love you always. I never
told any man that."

"I love you and I suppose I'll have to love you
always." *I feel like some question and answer game.*
I didn't love anybody. I only wanted Brett.
"It's a terrible business loving when you've
loved so many times that you know what it is."

"I don't know. *" said,"* (I've never loved a lot of people."

"Yes you have."

"Not the same way. Never had a chance."

"Let's not talk. Talking's all bilge. I'm
going away from you and then Michael's coming back."

"Why are you going away ?"

"Better for you. Better for me."

"When are you going ?"

"Soon as I can."

"Where ?"

"San Sebastian."

"Can't we go together ?"

"No. That would be a hell of an idea after we'd
just talked it out."

Hemingway's continued revising in search of an effective form for Jake and
Brett's statement of love is reflected even in the typescript of the novel. Even
here he had not yet achieved the effect he was seeking; he eventually restored
the deleted lines and deleted the lines that he had added to the typescript
(200-2-87).

By the time of the typescript second draft, Hemingway had cut the scene somewhat, yet he was still having some problems. Indeed, this section is notable as being the one scene that had been worked over in some detail in the typist's copy of the novel (item 200). A sense of fatality is introduced in this typed version. Instead of "I love you and I'll love you always" (194-2-28), Jake says, "I love you and *I suppose I'll have to love you* always" (200-2-87; my italics). Brett then replies, "It's *a terrible business* loving when you've loved so many times that you know what it is" (200-2-87; my italics). In that resort to a conventional idiom, Hemingway moved toward a more reserved Brett, a Brett who was more like the coolly controlled woman we see through so much of the published novel. But Jake was presented more petulantly in this draft; Hemingway underlined the irony of his "Not the same way" by adding a self-pitying second statement: "Never had a chance" (200-2-87).

But even these revisions did not satisfy him; on the typescript copy Hemingway crossed out the two lines that eventually appeared in print and added other material that underlined the ironic fatality of the lovers' predicament. The amended typescript (starting the quote a line or two earlier than above) reads this way:

> "It wouldn't be any good. I'll go if you like. But I couldn't live quietly in the country. Not with my own true love." *If I'd ever had one—"*
> "I know."
> ~~"Isn't it rotten? Isn't any use my telling you I love you."~~
> ~~"You know I love you."~~
> "I love you and I'll love you always. I never told any man that."
> "I love you and I suppose I'll have to love you always." *I felt like some question and answer game. I didn't love anybody. I only wanted Brett.*
> "It's a terrible business loving when you've loved so many times that you know what it is."
> "I don't know.*," I said,* "I've never loved a lot of people."
> "Yes you have."
> "Not the same way. Never had a chance."
> "Let's not talk. . . ."
> [200-2-87; Hemingway's handwritten additions to the typescript are in italics; his deletions are lined through.]

Eventually, in the draft from which the novel was set, Hemingway restored the two deleted sections of dialogue and pared away the rest. In the final version of the exchange, the pain *and* Jake and Brett's love are clearly presented; in this amended typescript version, Hemingway seems to have corrected the maudlin quality of the first-draft version by casting considerable doubt on the quality of the relationship between the two.

In the typescript draft quoted above, Brett's "If I'd ever had [a true love]—" suggests that she has never had a completely fulfilling relationship with a man, but it also suggests that Jake does not really love her. Such an implication is far different from the impression Hemingway eventually decided to convey, that Jake was emotionally Brett's true love though physically he could never be her lover. And while Jake's "I didn't love anybody. I only wanted Brett" suggests his intense feeling and confusion of emotion at being close to Brett, it again undercuts the sense that he is her "true love." Instead, in the typescript version, Jake seems much more like the Frederic Henry we see early in *A Farewell to Arms,* playing the word games that will let him take advantage of the need of a Catherine Barkley whom he does not yet love. (But here again, in Jake's mention of the "question and answer game," notice a return to the distrust of words that Hemingway eventually embodied in the scene's terse final version.)

All the conflicting elements of this typescript version of the scene—and similarly inappropriate elements in the notebook first draft—work against the effect that Hemingway finally decided upon. In this first private meeting between the lovers, he must establish clearly that Jake and Brett emotionally *are* lovers—he must strike a clear note that will resonate through the novel—and so he finally decides upon a restraint in the use of language which echoes and reinforces our perception of the inescapable restraints that fate has placed on the relationship between Brett and Jake.

THE SECOND SCENE: DISCUSSION OF THE DEATH
OF VICENTE GIRONES

In chapter 17 the discussion of the death of Vicente Girones is notable for several reasons. In terms of the structure of *The Sun Also Rises,* this conversation between Jake and a waiter in a café serves to underline the danger of the corrida, which Romero later so bravely faces, and also provides a needed balance: *The Sun Also Rises* is a book that quite frankly glorifies the values of the bullring. Yet such values would not necessarily be easily assimilated by all of Hemingway's readers, and certainly it would not be shared by all Spaniards, particularly by those Spaniards who avoid becoming caught up in the frenzy of the Pamplona fiesta. A balancing view is needed in order to complete the presentation—both to complete the portrait of the Spanish people and to establish a narrative distance between Jake Barnes, the aficionado narrator, and Ernest Hemingway, an author who was committed to making careful judgments.

Juxtaposed to the purely descriptive presentation of the frenzied, irrational running of the bulls, the conversation in the café—particularly the waiter's weary, wise commentary—allows Hemingway to complete his picture. Eventually, the waiter, who knows very well the cost of the festive corrida, is contrasted to Brett, who leaves the ear of the bull that killed Vicente Girones in the back of a drawer in the table beside her bed at the hotel. At this point in the book, contrary to some

The amateurs in the bullring at the end of the running of the bulls through the streets, 1925. Hemingway is wearing white pants (photo. no. EH 7891P, John F. Kennedy Library).

earlier impressions, it seems that she has not yet learned the values—either the aesthetic values of the experienced aficionado or the humane values expressed by the waiter.

The drafts of this scene represent an interesting departure from the novel's normal pattern of composition. Though the fifth notebook of the "first" draft includes a version of the scene which is fairly close to the published version, an earlier draft of the conversation exists on four loose sheets headed "insert Book V." It cannot be clearly stated just when this "pre-first-draft draft" was written. It may have been composed much earlier than the material around it and then saved to be copied into the notebook, but it seems much more likely, from an examination of internal evidence, that the four loose sheets were written in sequence with the material around them, that Hemingway simply didn't have his current notebook with him when he decided to work on that scene. The "insert Book V" heading suggests this, as does the fact that the 385 words of the insert draft end in the middle of a sentence at the top of the fourth page, as if Hemingway were following his practice of stopping when he knew what would come next. That page contains only one word, *the,* which comes at the end of the phrase "the coffin was carried to" (195a-3 and 4). Apparently, when Hemingway again had access to his notebook, he copied the scene into it, heightening and revising its language and completing the final sentence: "the coffin was carried to the railway. ~~the~~ station by ~~the~~ members of the different dancing societies of Pamplona" (194-5-39). Hemingway then continued to expand the description of the loading of the coffin. The section ends with a summary of the fate of the bull that killed Girones, which itself was killed by Pedro Romero, its ear ending up in the back of the drawer of Brett's bed table.

From the pre-notebook draft on loose sheets through the final published version, Hemingway's revision of this section was a matter of fine tuning for effect. Five versions of the scene exist—the pre-notebook draft, the notebook draft, the Hemingway typescript, the typescript from which type was set, and the very similar published version. Given that these last three versions are identical save for minor differences due to copyediting, this discussion will generally combine the last three and compare the three differing versions represented by the pre-notebook, the notebook, and the final drafts.

A simple word count of each version, beginning with Jake's "Back in the town I went to the café" (corresponding to *SAR,* p. 97) and running through the incomplete sentence at the top of the pre-notebook draft, reveals that the revision process operating in the section was far different from the one that Hemingway followed in his reworking of the Jake/Brett love scene. Running each word count to the same point in that incomplete final sentence, we discover that the final published version is no more than about fifteen words longer than the first draft (about 385 words in the pre-notebook draft compared to about 400 words in the published selection). Even the intermediate notebook version of the scene is only a few words longer (about 430 words).

Throughout the process of revision, only four very short sentences were cut, all from conversation; expansion of detail in the descriptive passages balanced these cuts and left the scene essentially unchanged in length and in structure—no elements were transposed. Except for one sentence that was added to the summary description of the life of Vicente Girones, new information was added only by additions to the existing structures—and only a little new information was added. The overall tone of the passage changed very little, if at all, in the revisions, yet the effect of the passage was considerably heightened as Hemingway worked to derive exact words and exact effects from his initial transcription. He worked to establish an absolute objectivity of narrative presentation, to reinforce the characterization of the waiter, and to match his language to the demands of his material.

Throughout the process of revision, Hemingway worked to achieve a precise and objective narration through the details that he presented. He often gave attention to minute details, as in the opening lines of the pre-notebook drafts, where he wrote, "Back in the town I went to the café to have another coffee and some buttered toast," then he crossed out "another" and wrote in "a second" (195a-1). The detail suggests just how early in the morning all of this has happened; it seems

Back in the town I went to the café
to have a second/another Coffee and some buttered
toast. The waiters were sweeping out and
mopping off the tables. One came up and took
my order.

"Anything happen at the encierro?" he
asked.

"I didn't see it all," I said. "One man
was badly cogida."

"Where."

"Here." I put my hands on the
small of my back and on my chest where it
looked as though the horn had come out.

The waiter nodded his head and swept
the crumbs from the table with his cloth.

"Badly cogida," he said and nodded
his head. "All for sport. All for pleasure."
He went away and came back with the
coffee and milk pots. He poured the milk and

This is a draft (see above and two following facsimile pages) of the scene in which Jake and the waiter discuss the goring of an aficionado during the running of the bulls. These three pages (and one word on a fourth page) were intensively sharpened in successive revisions, word by word (195-1, 2, and 3).

coffee from the long spouts into the big
cup. He nodded his head.

"Badly cogida through the back," he
said, putting the pots down on the table and
sitting in the chair opposite me. "A big horn
wound. All for fun you understand. Just
for fun. What do you think of that?"

"I don't know."

"That's the way. All for fun. Fun
you understand."

"You're not an aficionado?"

He shook his finger.

"What are bulls? Animals. That's not
fun. He stood up. "Right through the back.
A cornada right through the back. For fun -
you understand."

He shook his head and walked
away.

Two men coming from the Plaza
went by in the street. The waiter shouted to
them. They were grave looking. One shook his

③ insert

head.

"Muerto," he called. It was a bad sounding word.

The waiter nodded his head. The two men went on. They were evidently on some errand. The waiter came over to my table.

"You hear? Dead. He's dead. With a horn through him. All for fun. Muy flamenco. You like that?"

"It's bad. Very bad."

"Not for me," the waiter said. "No fun in that for me."

Later in the morning we learned that the man who had been killed was named Vicente Girones and came from near Tafalla. He was twenty eight years old and had a farm a wife and two children. His wife came in from Tafalla to get the body and after a service in the chapel of San Fermin the coffin was carried to the corrals. I left the fence and walked back toward the town. So did not want to see the amateurs with little padded horns. Not then.

Back in the town I went to the café to have a second coffee and some buttered toast. The waiters were sweeping out the café and mopping off the tables. One came up and took my order.

"Anything happen at the encierro?" he asked.

"I didn't see it all. One man was badly cogida."

"Where?"

"Here." I put one hand on the small of my back and the other on my chest, where I had looked as though the horn must have come through.

The waiter nodded his head and swept the crumbs from the table with his cloth.

"Badly cogida," he said. "All for

pleasure."

He went away and came back with the long handled coffee and milk pots. He poured the milk and the coffee from its long spouts into the boy cup. He nodded his head.

"Badly cogida through the back," he said, putting the pots down and sitting down in the chair opposite me. "A big horn wound. All for fun. Just for fun. What do you think of that?"

"I don't know."

"That's the way. All for fun. Fun. Fun, you understand."

"You're not an aficionado," said.

He shook his finger.

"What are bulls? Animals. Brute animals. That's not fun." He stood up and put his hand on the small of his back. "Right through the back. A cornada right through the back. For fun — you understand."

He shook his head and walked away. Two men were going by in the street. The

Hemingway first began to revise the account of Jake's conversation with the waiter as he copied it into his notebook (194-5-38).

almost tactile in its precision. A few lines later, Jake describes where Girones was gored: " 'Here.' I put my hands on the small of my back and on my chest where it looked as though the horn had come out" (195a-1). The use of touch and Jake's resorting to a demonstration make this form of presentation more real than a simple spoken description to the waiter could have been, but even in this passage, Hemingway was able to improve the precision of his presentation. He began to transfer the description word-for-word into his notebook: " 'Here.' I put m," stopping in the middle of "my." Then he lined through the *m* and revised in this manner: " 'Here.' I put m̶ *one hand on* the small of my back and *the other* on my chest where it had looked as though the horn must have come *through*" (194-5-38; my italics). Jake's posture is more accurately portrayed by the separate description of the position of each hand; the substitution of *through* for *out* much more accurately suggests the path of the horn, places greater emphasis on the terrible wound.

Throughout the scene, an ironic juxtapositon operates between the characters' consideration of Girones's goring and their ordinary interaction as a waiter and a customer in a café. As Hemingway made the first element of that pairing more immediate through his use of precise detail, he also balanced and offset the goring by revising his description of the café. Even in such a simple description as that of the waiter pouring milk and coffee into Jake's cup, Hemingway polished and refined his presentation; he worked in greater detail, repeated words for effect ("insistence"), and divided sentences into smaller units. Thus, in the pre-notebook draft, the waiter "went away and came back with the coffee and milk pots. He poured the milk and coffee from the long spouts into the big cup. He nodded his head" (195a-2 and 3). Here, already, Hemingway was slowing the tempo of presentation not only through the use of short, simple sentences but also by the repetition of the words *milk* and *coffee*. Even in this draft the pacing of the scene seems slow and deliberate, leading toward the waiter's stepping out of his role as servant, sitting down at the table, and discussing Girones's death with Jake.

In the notebook draft, Hemingway slowed the tempo even further, by separating the description of the waiter's deliberate actions from the immediately preceding presentation of his comments. Hemingway also increased his use of insistence, describing the pots as "long handled" to set up an echo in the following "long spouts" (194-5-38). In the final version, the precisely slowed and objective tone has been further reinforced by an introduction and by separating (by dividing one sentence into two) the *two streams* of coffee and milk from the act of pouring. The effect is thus slow—slow and deliberately observed; and every element is separately observed: "He went away and came back with the long-handled coffee and milk pots. He poured the milk and coffee. It came out of the long spouts in two streams into the big cup. The waiter nodded his head" (*SAR*, p. 197).

The result, seen in isolation from its context, may seem to epitomize the popular, often parodied conception of the "Hemingway style." The superficial aspects of this particular example of Hemingway's method are easily copied. But parodists and would-be Hemingways usually miss the purpose of the method. Instead of a haunting *insistence,* they often produce only a superficial repetition. They use short sentences, not for their effect on tempo and their concentration on the moment, but only because short sentences are an easily identifiable (or, more often misidentified) element of Hemingway's prose. But here Hemingway led toward the waiter's later comments and also suggested something of Jake's state of mind, as Jake concentrates on simple elements of everyday life as a refuge from the horror of the thought of the goring.

In the ensuing paragraphs of description, Hemingway continued to revise in a similar manner. He worked by means of insistence, particularly the insistence of the waiter's reiterated (seven times in the final version; eight times in the drafts) ironic use of *fun* to describe the actions that led up to the death of Girones: ''All for fun. Just for fun. . . . All for fun. Fun, you understand'' (*SAR,* p. 197). Other insistent repetitions include the use of *bad* and *badly cogido* (''gored''), the repetition in conversation and in the gestures of both Jake and the waiter of the *back* as the site of Girones's wound, and the waiter's repeated emphasis on the bulls as ''Animals. Brute animals'' (*SAR,* p. 197). Some other examples of insistent repetition even cross the Spanish/English language barrier, combining repetition with an in-context explanation of the Spanish: for example, *badly cogido* and *cornada/a big horn wound; muerto/dead;* and *es muy flamenco/it's bad.* Only two Spanish words are not echoed in the English text—*encierro* and *aficionado;* but both have already been explained earlier in the novel.

While all these repetitions had their roots in the pre-notebook draft of the scene, Hemingway's revisions operated in most cases to point up their importance. (But in several instances he worked to reduce the impact of such insistence in order to balance the overall tone of the passage.) The waiter's echo of Jake's gesture, touching his back to indicate where the horn went in, was introduced in the notebook draft; in the final draft it has completely replaced a gesture that comes a line or two earlier, where the waiter shakes his finger at Jake. The sketchy first-draft version was:

> ''You're not an aficionado?''
> He shook his finger.
> ''What are bulls? Animals. That's not fun.'' He stood up. ''Right through the back. A cornada right through the back. For fun—you understand.'' [195a-2]

In the notebook draft, in addition to introducing the waiter's echo of Jake's gesture, Hemingway also increased his insistent repetition of *bulls/animals:*

> ''You're not an aficionado,'' I said.
> He shook his finger.
> ''What are bulls? Animals. ~~Dirty~~ Brute animals. That's not fun.''
> He stood up and put his hand on the small of his back. ''Right through the back. A cornada right through the back. For fun—you understand.'' [194-5-38]

But while that eloquent repetition of the gesture has been introduced, the overall effect of revision is not entirely complete. The introduction of the speaker identification, "I said," is not necessary for the careful reader—because, logically, only Jake could have made the statement about being an aficionado. Along with a number of other such identifications, the "I said" was deleted from the final novel, and the statement was returned to the form of a question, as in the first draft. (Indeed, one of the more consistent changes that Hemingway made in his revision of the entire manuscript of *The Sun Also Rises* was the deletion of such identifications of speakers throughout the novel.)

In this intermediate version, also, the waiter's character is not conveyed as being the same as in the final draft. Here he seems petulant and irascible rather than wearied and wise; the finger shaking was too quick a movement to fit the character that Hemingway was drawing, and the phrase "*Dirty* Brute animals" (my italics) was too vehemently emotional and unthinking to be appropriate. Both elements were deleted in the final version of the scene, as was the first reference to *fun*, leaving the waiter's rhetorical question and answer to be followed by the more appropriate gesture. The tone of this section becomes consistent with the slow, somber effect of the entire scene:

> "You're not an aficionado?"
> "Me? What are bulls? Animals. Brute animals." He stood up and put his hand on the small of his back. "Right through the back. A cornada right through the back. For fun—you understand." [*SAR*, pp. 197–98]

Objectivity and attention to the moment continued to characterize Hemingway's revisions of the scene. A late revision, for example, added the information that as the waiter walks away from Jake, he carries the coffeepots. In draft one, the two men who announce the death of Girones are identified as "coming from the Plaza" (195a-2), but in the notebook draft, Hemingway altered that detail—they became "men going by in the street" (194-5-38). That is, Hemingway carefully limited his narrator to the information that was available to him at the immediate moment; in recounting the story, Jake might well identify the men as having come from the bullring; but while he is sitting in the café, at the moment when he first sees them, he cannot know where they have come from. Hemingway took the same kind of care when he described Girones later in the section.

In the first draft, Jake tells us that later in the morning he learned Girones's name (up to this point he had not been identified by name) and then continues to tell about Girones's hometown and life. But in the notebook draft, as he expanded the description of Girones, Hemingway was careful to identify the source of information other than his name: "*The next day in the paper we read* that he was twenty eight years old and had a farm, a wife and two children. He had continued to come to the Fiestas each year after he had married" (194-5-39; my emphasis).

The precision of this objective presentation continued as Hemingway completed the scene, but in the notebook second draft, Hemingway added the comment about Girones's continuing to attend the fiestas even after his marriage. This sentence is the least easily ascribable, with regard to source, of any sentence in the entire section—it could be based on information that Jake had gleaned from the newspaper account or perhaps a fact that he had learned in conversation. The ambiguity, however, serves functionally to blend in the newspaper information with the following description of the funeral procession as Jake observes it. Jake gives us an apparently simple narration of "the facts" of that funeral; yet in revising it, Hemingway tuned Jake's narration to continue the somber tone that has earlier been established. Thus, in the pre-notebook draft, Girones's wife "came in from Tafalla to get the body" (195a-3). In the notebook and in subsequent drafts, she comes "the next day . . . to be with the body" (194-5-39); the change from the active "get" to the passive "be with" again slows the scene, as does the introduction of an intervening day. The passive verb also serves to characterize the hopelessness of what has happened—nothing can be done about it.

Again slowing the scene, Hemingway first described the funeral procession in a summary sort of way, noting that "the coffin was carried to the railway." He then expanded his description—it was "carried to the railway. the station by the members of the different dancing societies of Pamplona" (194-5-39; Hemingway's deletions). Even that description has been expanded by the time of the final draft—the coffin is carried "by members of the dancing and drinking society of Tafalla." And behind the coffin walk Girones's wife and children, followed by "members of the dancing and drinking societies of Pamplona, Estella, Tafalla and Sanguesa" (*SAR*, p. 198).

Hemingway worked toward ever finer gradations of apparently objective description. As the apparent narrator, Jake tells us nothing that he does not observe himself. Hemingway even cut an earlier judgment by Jake, when he first uses the word *muerto* ("dead"): "it was a bad sounding word" (195a-3 and 194-5-39). Here, in opposition to the presentation of opinion in equal parts with information, which so often characterizes Jake Barnes as narrator (as in the description of Robert Cohn in the published first chapter), Hemingway has made Jake a perceptually sensitive yet objective narrator. Through the interplay of juxtaposing the calm café scene with the discussion of the death of Vicente Girones, through the intensive use of an echoing insistence, and through the slowing of tempo in intensive description, Hemingway has developed the possibilities of his first draft by revising and thus producing a counter to the philosophy of the aficionado, which operates through the sorts of devices that are most often associated with poetry. Through a careful attention to each element within the scene—which often results in having words, phrases, and entire sentences serve several functions, Hemingway achieved his effects without any appreciable change in the length of the passage. His first draft was compact and effective; his final draft is even more evocative as a result of his continued attention to craft.

THE THIRD SCENE: ROMERO IN THE BULLRING

In chapter 18 of the published version of *The Sun Also Rises*, Jake, Brett, and Bill watch as Romero holds center stage in the Pamplona bullring, fighting two bulls. This corrida takes place on the day after Robert Cohn has beaten up Jake and Romero; but in the bullring, Romero asserts his artistry as a matador in spite of his injuries—Romero "was wiping all that out now" (*SAR*, p. 219). In a sense, Romero also is wiping out the death of Vicente Girones, reasserting man's control over brute nature as he fights his second bull of the afternoon, the bull that had killed Girones in the running that morning.

In the final version of the scene, Romero has become the perfect matador, intelligently handling his first bull, which is half blind and cowardly and therefore far less predictable to Romero than a brave, unblemished animal would be. With his second bull, which is brave and whole yet also proved dangerous by killing Girones, Romero produces a perfect bullfight, a bullfight in which he reaches the artistic perfection that Hemingway later so carefully elucidated in *Death in the Afternoon*. Romero returns to the style of the classic corrida, completely dominating the bull in pass after pass and finally killing it in the style of the great classical matador Pedro Romero, after whom Hemingway named his character. The Romero of *The Sun Also Rises* echoes the historical Romero, killing *recibiéndo* ("receiving"), while he is standing still and provoking the bull to charge him, rather than taking the far safer course and running in toward the bull in order to kill him. As Hemingway described the corrida, the death of the bull comes as the perfect climax to the description of the bullfight; it also works structurally as an antidote to the sordid happenings of the preceding scenes and chapters.

In its earlier versions, the scene also works effectively, but not as effectively. It did not concentrate so completely on Romero, nor did it lead so directly toward the climactic death of Romero's second bull. And in the early draft, that death is described in a completely different manner: Romero (who was called Guerrita in the notebook draft of the scene) follows the modern style of moving in toward the bull; the climactic moment is not so perfect, nor is it so perfectly presented, since Jake intrudes as narrator as he offers a sort of running commentary on his reactions to Romero's actions.

In revision, then, Hemingway worked to reduce intrusions in the narrative and to produce a clean movement toward the scene's climax in the killing of Romero's second bull; he was careful to keep the scene focused more directly on Romero than on Jake's and Brett's reactions to the corrida. He worked sometimes through the sort of intensive revision that characterized his reworking of the conversation in the café between Jake and the waiter, by finely tuning the existing material. In places he deleted a good deal of Jake's exposition and commentary, following his iceberg principle: such deletion became particularly important in submerging the impressions of the two other matadors and the four other bulls involved in the bullfight. Hemingway also substituted new material in place of less effective writing and added a good deal of description. In these revisions he re-created the corrida as it occurs, moment by moment.

In both drafts of the scene, Jake fills a dual role as narrator and expert commentator on the bullfight; his commentary, which indicates that he is at least outwardly calm, contrasts with the role here given to Brett, who is tensely silent and nearly invisible throughout. In his description of the early course of the corrida, before Romero fights his first bull, Jake is most clearly the expert commentator, as he carefully analyzes Belmonte, the faded great matador whose return from retirement is ruined by the presence of a new young matador who is just coming into his prime: Romero. In his description of Belmonte, Jake concentrates on all the decisions that the old matador has made before entering the ring, particularly the choice of easy bulls with small horns, which make Belmonte's task easier and detract from the moments of greatness he still achieves: the greatness "had been discounted and sold in advance" (*SAR*, p. 216).

But as Guerrita/Romero comes to the center of the scene, Hemingway changes the tone and nature of Jake's narration; from a generalized analysis spiced by the occasional detail of Belmonte's actions we move into a moment-by-moment description of Romero's work in the ring. This immediate description—in its final form—is very seldom interrupted by Jake's explanations. And these explanations do not intrude; they are generally introduced only when the reader needs additional information in order to comprehend the significance of the immediate action, as when Jake interprets the course of the bullfight.

A number of revisions serve to strengthen the focus in to the moment, working through added detail and careful pacing. The first-draft version of Guerrita's first *quite* (the leading of the bull to and then away from the mounted picador) works this way:

> Guerrita flicked his cape so the color caught the bulls eye and the bull charged with the reflex, charged and found not color but a white horse and a man leaning far down shot the ~~stick~~ steel point of the long hickory shaft into the bulls shoulder and pulled his horse sideways as he pivoted on the pic, enforcing the iron into the bulls shoulder ~~and~~ cutting him down to size for Belmonte. [194-6-14]

The sentence moves with a sense of rushing motion which echoes the movement of the bull, but at the same time a good deal of information is offered about the way a bullfighter works. The bull's charge is a matter of *reflex;* the picador does not deliver a clean wound but moves sideways to make a tear as he works to prepare the bull for Belmonte—perhaps doing more than he should ("cutting him down to size"). Yet in revising, Hemingway achieved a more precise description. The first revisons, written into the notebook above the lines, offer additional information and also slow the rushing movement at the end of the sentence, where the bull is caught and held by the *pic:* "he pivoted on the pic, *making a wound,* enforcing the iron into the bulls shoulder -and; cutting him *further* down to size for Belmonte" (194-6-14; additions italicized).

The final version of the bull's charge is handled with infinite precision. First, the single sentence is split into two sentences; Hemingway separates Guerrita/ Romero's action from the bull's response—the flick of the cape and the bull's reflexive charge are not one action, but two; and the moment between action and reaction is reflected in the pause as a result of the period. The color of the cape becomes "the flash of color," again emphasizing the momentary nature of the action; "the hump of muscle on the bull's shoulder" is identified as the target for the *pic,* thus coming closer to suggesting the purpose for the picador's action. (As long as the muscle in the neck remains strong, the bull can hold his head so high that the matador will inevitably be gored as he attempts a killing sword thrust over the horns. The wound made by the *pic* helps to weaken that muscle.) The picador is no longer portrayed as cutting the bull down to size but, more immediately, as "making him bleed for Belmonte."

The final tempo of the description derives from all these revisions: quick (the movement of Romero's cape); quick (the bull's reflexive charge); then slow (the wounding of the bull by the picador, which is restated in four different ways):

> Romero flicked his cape so the color caught the bull's eye. The bull charged with the reflex, charged, and found not the flash of color but a white horse, and a man leaned far over the horse, shot the steel point of the long hickory shaft into the hump of muscle on the bull's shoulder, and pulled his horse sideways as he pivoted on the pic, making a wound, enforcing the iron into the bull's shoulder, making him bleed for Belmonte. [*SAR,* p. 216]

In revising, Hemingway also slowed the ending of this description by two other devices. He introduced an insistent repetition of the word *horse,* adding the second of the three mentions of the horse in the passage quoted above. He also helped to hold the moment by introducing a paragraph pause just after the quoted description, before going on to describe the breaking off of the contact between the picador and the bull. This paragraph break, which did not exist in the notebook draft, serves to slow the reader's movement from the description just as a line ending or a stanza ending would slow the tempo of movement in a work of poetry. The moment is emphasized and made important by this rhythmic attention as well as by the careful attention paid to the details of the action.

The process of refinement by which Hemingway handled the above description of the bull's charge toward the picador included some substitution of elements. For example, the highly descriptive interpretation of the action by Jake, "making him bleed for Belmonte," was substituted for the ironic cliché "cutting him further down to size.'' That same sort of substitution of the descriptive phrase for the cliché was made elsewhere in the scene and can often be seen elsewhere in the drafts of *The Sun Also Rises.*

A few lines after the picador section, Romero passes the bull, taking him out away from the horse and rider and completing the *quite.* In the first version of this *quite,* Romero (here called Guerrita, again) offers the cape. ''The bull wanted it and came and Guerrita did not sidestep,'' Hemingway began the description, then immediately lined through the ''did not sidestep'' and continued with ''moved one step to the side and swung the cape'' (194-6-14). Here Jake is interpreting the action for us—but not interpreting very eloquently—in the cliché idiom ''the bull wanted it,'' and the statement throws the focus away from the moment. In making revisions, Hemingway turned away from Jake's interpretation and toward a direct re-creation of the moment in careful description. He also returned to that lined-out first idea (that Guerrita/Romero did not sidestep) as he built toward Romero's *recibiéndo* killing of his second bull and then returned in the following sentence to the movement of the cape:

> The bull's tail went up and he charged, and Romero moved his arms ahead of the bull, wheeling, his feet firmed. The dampened, mud-weighted cape swung open and full as a sail fills, and Romero pivoted with it just ahead of the bull. [*SAR,* p. 217]

In ensuing sentences, Hemingway purposely moved toward Jake's description and interpretation of the action, but he did so only after he had completed describing one pass, after a context had been established for that interpretation. In the final version, he let stand a second use of ''the bull wanted it,'' leading into the more generalized description of five more passes of the bull, which leads in turn into Jake's analysis of the extreme technical difficulties that Romero faces as he works with his own first bull, the bull with impaired vision.

Hemingway, of course, is meeting his own technical difficulty here: he could not describe every pass that Romero made with each bull without producing anything but a hopelessly long muddle; no matter how precisely he controlled each description, any presentation of each immediate moment in the bullfight would have become impossibly long. Instead, all those moments that he did *not* describe became a part of the seven-eighths of the descriptive iceberg, and Jake's commentary must help to bring the reader through the scene by suggesting the quality of each individual moment in such statements as this, made in reference to Romero's handling of the half-blind bull: ''It was not brilliant bull fighting it was only perfect bullfighting'' (194-6-15). Of course, in revising, Hemingway separated the two ideas, letting each stand as a separate sentence: ''It was not brilliant bull-fighting. It was only perfect bull-fighting'' (*SAR,* p. 217).

Throughout the scene, Hemingway continued to break sentences into smaller units, slowing Jake's more generalized descriptions, much as he had earlier slowed and controlled the tempo of the immediate description of one moment as Romero began the first *quite*. This sort of process is particularly obvious in the revisions that Hemingway made as he moved from the presentation of that first *quite* to Jake's summary description of how the five succeeding passes appeared. In the first draft the effect of the description is somewhat diffuse, almost hazy: "Each time [he] let the bull come so close that the man and the bull and the cape that filled out ~~ahead~~ pivoting ahead of the bull all were one mass. and it was all so slow and so controlled" (194-6-14 and 15). In his revision, Hemingway substituted Romero as the active subject of the sentence in place of the much more abstract "each time"; he carefully tuned his language to convey exact images, substituting "pass so close" for "come so close" in describing the path of the bull; he ended the first sentence with the image of matador and bull as "one sharply etched mass" and then followed that sharp image with his sentence of generalization: "Each time he let the bull pass so close that the man and the bull and the cape that filled and pivoted ahead of the bull were all one sharply etched mass. It was all so slow and so controlled" (*SAR*, p. 217). The single image eloquently conveys the essence of each pass, and Jake's comment binds the whole action together.

In this primarily descriptive scene, even the few lines of conversation that Hemingway included moved from diffuse to more direct forms as he completed his revision. In the notebook draft, Jake and Duff/Brett's discussion of the half-blind bull rambles, much as conversation rambled in their early love scene: Hemingway told more than he needed to. And as the profusion of words undercuts the intense emotion of that early draft of the love scene, in this conversation the words work to draw attention away from the real central concern of the speaking characters, that the matador is in great danger:

> Nothing very fine could happen with a bull with defective vision but the President would not order him ~~changed.~~ replaced.
> "Why don't they change him?" Duff asked.
> "They've paid for him. They don't want to lose their money."
> "One would think they'd have to give another for a blind bull."
> "Yes," I said. "But he may have done it banging against the wall of the chiquero before he came out."
> "It's hardly fair for Guerrita."
> "Well," I said, "the crowd give him credit. Watch how he handles a bull that cant see the capes."
> "It's the sort of thing I don't like to see."
> Duff was right. [194-6-15]

In this early version of the conversation, Jake was being too fair to the officials of the bullring. His explanation of the interests of the officials and of the breeder who delivered the bull was eminently rational and fair, but it had nothing to do with what was going on in the ring. Here Jake overstepped his proper function as expert guide to the bullfight and introduced wholly extraneous information rather than information and an interpretation that would heighten the reader's appreciation of what Guerrita/Romero was accomplishing.

the man and the bull and the cape that filled out ahead pivoting ahead of the bull all were one thing and it was all so slow and so controlled. It was as though he were robbing the bull to sleep. He made four veronicas like that and finished with a half veronica that turned his back on the bull and came away toward the applause, his hand on his hip, his cape on his arm and the bull watching his back going away.

In his arm... levels he was perfect. His first bull did not see well. After the first two passes with the cape Guerrita knew was suspected... worked accordingly it was not brilliant bull fighting. It was only perfect bull fighting. Wanted the bull clean of the crowd... made a great four... Nicardo... four... once happen with a sort... with a — defective vision first the bull...

President would not order him changed... replied.
"Why don't they change him?"
Dull asked.
"They've paid for him. They don't want to lose their money."
... we would think that they have to give another... for a blind bull.
"Yes," I said. "But he may have done it ... against the wall, the ... before he came out.
"It's lardh... often for Guerita.
"Maybe que handles a bull
him credit. Water, how he handles a bull that can't see the cape..."
"It's the sort of thing ... I don't like to see ... nine ... they ... from anyone who don't know enough. With a bull who cannot see the cape or the ... scarlet flannel of the muleta Guerita had to make the bull ... with his body. He had to get so close that the bull saw his body and charged it for the Guerita would ... shift the

Hemingway apparently recognized this flaw and moved to correct it. As he worked over the notebook draft, he first added Jake's ironically restrained summary comment, "It was not nice to watch if you cared anything about the person who was doing it." This line replaced the simple judgment "Duff was right" and moved the scene a step closer to the sort of immediate impression of danger that is required. As in the earlier love scene, Hemingway completed his revision by paring away extraneous conversation until the few remaining lines suggested the apprehension with which both Jake and Brett were watching the matador's work with the defective bull. (Throughout the description of the bullfight, it is only in the three lines of her dialogue that were retained in this section that Brett speaks at all. Elsewhere she does not respond to Jake's comments on the course of the corrida nor does she even later answer Romero's question "You liked it?" as he hands her the ear cut from his second bull, though by that point the tension of the fight has been dispelled enough so that she could smile (*SAR*, p. 221).

The final version of the exchange between Jake and Brett completely omits any discussion of the justification for the officials' allowing the use of a defective bull: instead, they are implicitly judged as Jake comments that they didn't want to lose their money. And Jake's tension is seen as he attempts to divert Brett from thinking about the danger to Romero, asking her to concentrate on Romero's technique as he works skillfully with the half-blind bull:

Nothing very fine could happen with a bull that could not see the lures, but the President would not order him replaced.
    "Why don't they change him?" Brett asked.
    "They've paid for him. They don't want to lose their money."
    "It's hardly fair to Romero."
    "Watch how he handles a bull that can't see the color."
    "It's the sort of thing I don't like to see."
    It was not nice to watch if you cared anything about the person who was doing it. With the bull who could not see the colors of the capes, or the scarlet flannel of the muleta, Romero had to make the bull consent with his body. [*SAR*, p. 217]

Conversation was pared down again later in the scene: Hemingway eliminated Jake's comment to Bill on the killing of Romero's first bull, the difficult, half-blind animal. " 'That's not a stylish way to kill them,' I said, 'But it's one way' " (194-6-17). A few lines later he reduced the overheard exchange at the *barrera* between Romero and his sword handler. In the first draft the conversation was handled this way:

    "Bad one," said the sword handler.
    "He made me sweat," said Guerrita. He wiped off his face and put on his hat.

"Nice estocade," the sword handler handed over the water jug. Guerrita wiped his lips.

"Not so good," he took the cape. "All right if you like it." [194-6-17]

In the revised version, less is said, but more of the tension that Romero felt while killing the bull is conveyed:

"Bad one," said the sword-handler.

"He made me sweat," said Romero. He wiped off his face. The sword-handler handed him the water-jug. Romero wiped his lips. It hurt him to drink out of the jug. He did not look up at us. [*SAR*, p. 219]

Both in the conversation between Guerríta and the sword handler and in Jake's comment to Bill, Hemingway was working to reduce the attention directly paid to the difficulty of Guerrita/Romero's achievement with the defective animal. Or at least he was working to underplay the cues he offers to the reader, particularly since in the subsequent description, Romero's performance with the half-blind bull would be juxtaposed with the presentation of his achievements with his second bull, a perfect one.

Jake's first-draft comment on the lack of style in the killing of the first bull is at least partially accurate, since necessity overrode all other considerations, including style, in the working of the defective animal. But in at least two ways the comment is inappropriate to the overall impression that Hemingway seems to be striving for. First, the emphasis on style seems to imply that Guerrita is consciously attempting to project a certain style rather than letting whatever style he has result from his careful work with the bull. That is, in Jake's comment, style is treated as being ornamental rather than organic. Second, in making that comment, Jake undercuts his own credibilty as an expert narrator. His comments "That's not a stylish way to kill them. . . . But it's one way" are a little too ironic and balanced, a little too like the sort of comment we might expect from a witty member of the uncomprehending "Biarritz bull-fight experts" whom Jake so scorns a page or so earlier in the novel (*SAR*, pp. 217–18).

The tone of Guerrita/Romero's "Not so good. . . . All right if you like it" is similarly inappropriate in its context; it is too much the sort of cynical, terse comment one might expect from a matador who was more seasoned and worn down than the nineteen-year-old Romero. This first-draft comment offers the reader no new information—the difficulty of the bull that Romero has worked with has already been carefully demonstrated, and Hemingway's substitution of details of Romero's actions at the *barrera* functions more appropriately. In these substitutions for the terse comments of the first-draft version, Hemingway has chosen to emphasize the physical difficulty for Romero of having to work after the beating he has received from Cohn—"It hurt him to drink." Hemingway also emphasized the isolation (at least partly a chosen isolation) of the matador, who will not look up at Jake and Brett.

In the concluding sections of Jake's description of the bullfight, differences between the first draft and the final version become more and more obvious, as Hemingway worked with the heavy emphasis on Jake's analysis of the action and transformed it into a more direct presentation that was rooted in the immediate moment. In the notebook draft, as the bullfight moves toward Romero's climactic killing of his second bull, Jake returns to the analysis of the merits of the three matadors with which he led into the presentation of Romero's actions in the ring.

In Jake's analyses in the first draft, he sometimes seems to hover on the edge of becoming an omniscient narrator. The conversation between Romero and his sword handler at the *barrera* seems to verge on being information that Jake could not have known; but since Jake and his friends are sitting in front-row seats, they might have been able to overhear them. Nevertheless, Jake could not have known Romero's thoughts. Speaking of Romero's second bull, Jake tells us: "This bull made him Guerrita happy again. . . . incidentally he destroyed Marcial's triumph. That was only incidental. He did not care anything about Marcial or Marcial's triumph. . . . He was himself and he had the greatness and he felt whole again inside" (194-6-18).

These statements, like many other statements in the first drafts, seem to represent the direct voice of Ernest Hemingway showing through the screen of Jake Barnes, narrator, which had not yet been adequately developed. This material seems to serve as Hemingway's note to himself in the process of developing one element of the finished book, as did other such material that I discussed earlier. In this case the element is character, and the first-draft treatment is not unlike Hemingway's first-draft treatments of the idea of the hero and the importance of the fiesta as a catalytic agent in the action of the novel: Hemingway established a clear idea of what he wanted to present in his first draft, and then he modified his method of presentation to conform to the overall narrative scheme of the finished novel.

In this section of the bullfight scene, Hemingway moved away from the omniscient stance to an analysis closely based on things that Jake could himself have observed. This movement took place even in the first draft; just after the section of "omniscient analysis," Hemingway restated the ideas in that section in more objective form:

> During his first bull his hurt face had been very noticeable. Everything he did showed it. all the concentration of the awkwardly delicate working with the bull that could not see well brought it out. It was the a the the such beaten face of a fighter coming out of the side entrance of the g old garden after a hard fight. The fight with Cohn had not touched his spirit. That in the end was what destroyed Cohn. But his face had been smashed and his body hurt. He was wiping all that out now. Each thing he did with the bull wiped that out a little. As he worked with the bull he wiped all that away. It was a good bull, a big bull and with horns and it turned quickly and re-charged easily and surely. He was what Guerrita wanted in bulls. When he had finished with the muleta the crowd made him go on and he went on. [194-6-18]

This passage illustrates Hemingway's movement toward an "objective" presentation. After making an analysis of Guerrita (Romero) in comparison to the older matador, Marcial, Hemingway tried to convey the essence of his analysis more directly by referring to events in the bullfight (194-6-18).

Here, Jake's judgments—namely, that Romero's spirit was untouched and that with this second, a perfect, bull he was "wiping out" the damage to his body—do not seem to be the result of an omniscient consciousness. Instead, they seem to be judgments made on the basis of Jake's observations of how Romero worked with his bulls, and so these judgments seem to be more appropriate to the narrative scheme of the novel. Predictably, Hemingway's later revisions eliminated the preceding "omniscient" analyses of Romero/Guerrita, as compared to Marcial, and concentrated on integrating this more objective section into the flow of the description of the bullfight.

Hemingway carefully excised those parts of Jake's description and interpretation which move beyond the immediate context of the corrida. The metaphoric statement identifying Romero's face as that of "a fighter coming out of the side entrance of the old garden after a hard fight" certainly evokes a precise image, yet its reference leaves the framework of the bullring. When he revised, Hemingway deleted it. Jake's reference to the fight with Robert Cohn is, of course, relevant to Romero's accomplishments in the ring; therefore Hemingway retained it. But he cut the judgment that Romero's spirit, untouched by Cohn's blows, "in the end was what destroyed Cohn." That judgment offered little new information: Hemingway had already presented Cohn's defeat, and the reference to Cohn at this point again detracted from the immediacy of Jake's narrative involvement in describing the bullfight.

Hemingway also worked to reduce to a more manageable level his use of insistent repetition. In the notebook draft, he repeated three times in a row the idea of "wiping away" the effects of the fight:

> He was wiping all that out now. Each thing he did with the bull wiped that out a little. As he worked with the bull he wiped all that away. [194-6-18]

In the final draft he had cut the three mentions to two:

> He was wiping all that out now. Each thing that he did with this bull wiped that out a little cleaner. [*SAR*, p. 219]

The emphasis gained by repetition has been retained in the double repetition; perhaps some of the slowing effect of a triple repetition has been lost in the revision, but here (as elsewhere in the description of the bullfight) Hemingway again slowed the rhythm of the presentation by making other revisions. This short sentence illustrates the process: "When he had finished with the muleta the crowd made him go on and he went on" (194-6-18). In his final version of the sentence, set as the beginning of a new paragraph, Hemingway added a good deal of new information, which is italicized: "When he had finished *his work* with the muleta *and was ready to kill*, the crowd made him go on. *They did not want the bull killed yet, and they did not want it to be over.* Romero-and he went on" (*SAR*, p. 219). The single sentence has become three, and new insistences have been added, again slowing the tempo of presentation: Hemingway has reintroduced the idea of

Romero's *work* in the ring and has also introduced an insistent repetition of the crowd's desire to have the bullfight go on, which is restated twice after the first draft's "the crowd made him go on" (194-6-18). At the end of the paragraph that this passage begins, he added yet another repetition of the idea: "The crowd did not want it ever to be finished" (*SAR*, p. 220).

The most remarkable revisions in this corrida scene came in the description of its climactic moment, Romero's killing of the second bull, which is described in the long paragraph that fills most of page 220 of *The Sun Also Rises*. Here Hemingway made a very considerable substitution of material, replacing the first-draft description—in which Romero kills in the manner of modern bullfighters—with a completely different section, in which Romero kills *recibiéndo,* using the technique of his namesake from the classic era of the corrida.

In the first-draft version, Romero's actions are elegantly controlled, yet the description is of the modern style of killing (which Hemingway later termed "decadent" in *Death in the Afternoon*), and Jake Barnes's narrative voice seems fairly intrusive. Hemingway here continued to use the analytic tone he had been at such pains to integrate as unobtrusively as possible into a narration that was concentrating on immediate moments. In the first-draft version, Jake describes the position of the bull and then continues with an analysis that includes information seemingly drawn from Romero's consciousness:

> Then the bull was calmed and squared away to be killed and Guerrita killed directly below us. He killed not as he had been forced to by the last bull, but as he wanted to. [194-6-18]

The tone of that judgment—that Romero killed "as he wanted to"—is continued in the notebook version in a description that is heavily dependent on Jake's knowledge of bullfighting. Romero killed

> as he wanted to. Not blinding the bull with the muleta but only indicating to him how he should go, executing perfectly the three tempos of the Volapié the ~~most beautiful~~ best thing I know to watch in bull fighting. ~~After~~ He profiled and sighted along the blade, ~~he~~ made the three steps, the one that takes the measure, the one that gets there and then the one that carries the left shoulder forward and drives in the sword, the left hand crossed in front of the chest gives the bull the sortie with the muleta and the swordsman, having been one with the bull is then alone, the bull having broken the figure himself because the man has planned it so.
>
> Handkerchiefs were waving all over the stands ~~and~~ before the bull was dead. [194-6-18 and 19]

The first difficulty with this description was, of course, that Jake was telling how any skilled matador would kill, given a brave and responsive bull. The tone is somewhat idealized, and the matador's actions are elegant. But the actions could be those of any fine matador; therefore too little of the description works to set Romero apart. Indeed, the idealization of the description is an idealization of

The first version of the killing of Romero's second bull. In revision, Hemingway particularized this scene (194-6-19).

abstraction, as if the narrator had generalized from the best work he had seen in the bullring. In making revisions on the notebook page, Hemingway added Jake's comment that the *volapié* is "the best thing *I know to watch* in bullfighting," not that Romero's execution of the maneuver is the finest that Jake has ever seen. The three steps of the *volapié* seem similarly abstracted in Jake's analysis. During the description of the kill, it is not Guerrita or Romero who acts, but the swordsman, the man, part of the figure formed by man and bull. The implication seems to be that in this confrontation an archetypal man is meeting an archetypal bull. That implication is not entirely incongruous, given that in the perfection of Guerrita/ Romero's work and the perfection of the second bull's reactions, an archetypal confrontation between man and beast may be developing. But in this first-draft description the archetypal floated too far away from the actual. The concentration on the immediate moment has been lost in a too-great idealization, as has the triumph of Romero in fighting superbly despite the physical battering that he had received earlier.

In his typescript draft of the scene (198), Hemingway had solved the difficulties of the scene by completely replacing Jake's analytically idealized description with a newly created sequence of events in which Romero remains directly at the center of attention. In this new sequence, the element of idealization is closely tied to Romero, who achieves his triumph in controlling the difficult and dangerous technique of killing *recibiéndo*. In this description there are no references to the entire ritual of bullfighting but only a precisely controlled description of several moments in one bullfight:

> The bull was squared on all four feet to be killed and Romero killed directly below us. He killed not as he had been forced to by the last bull, but as he wanted to. He profiled directly in front of the bull, drew the sword out of the folds of the muleta and sighted along the blade. The bull watched him. Romero spoke to the bull and tapped one of his feet. The bull charged and Romero waited for the charge, the muleta held low, sighting along the blade his feet firm. Then without taking a step forward he became one with the bull, the sword was in high between the shoulders, the bull had followed the low swung flannel, that disappeared as Romero stepped clear and it was over. [198-4-154]

Here, nothing floats away from the reality of the moment. Each action that is described is the action of one man and one bull; the climactic moment of the bullfight is no longer idealized by the narrator's interposition. Rather, the action is ideal—one fine example of the artistry possible in the bullfight. Each movement is carefully paced in description, in longer, fluid sentences that describe Romero's preparations to receive the bull and lead to the terse, four-word description "The bull watched him." From that still moment of watching, Romero's two actions— speaking to the bull and tapping his foot—break the stillness and lead to the resolution in two longer sentences, the first describing Romero's unmoving wait for the charge and the second portraying the killing of the bull.

And each pass as it reached the summit gave you a sudden ache

inside . The crowd did not want it ever to be finished .

~~Then~~ The bull was squared on all four ~~legs~~ feet to be

killed and Romero killed directly below us . He killed not as he had

been forced to by the last bull, but as he wanted to . He profiled

directly in front of the bull , drew the sword out of the folds of the

muleta and sighted along the blade . The bull watched him . Romero

spoke to the bull and tapped one of his feet . The bull charged

and Romero waited for the charge , the muleta held low , sighting along *to circle and*

the blade his feet firm . Then without taking a step forward he

became one with the bull , the sword ~~was~~ was in high between the

shoulders , the bull had followed the low swung flannel , that *swung from*

disappeared as Romero stepped clear and it was over . The bull/went   hesitated/then

down on his knees and Romero's older brother leaned forward behind him

and drove a short knife into the bull's neck at the base of the

horns . The first time he missed.~~then~~ the bull went over ,~~haunned~~   He drove the knife in again and

~~shuddering backw~~ twitching and rigid . Romero's ~~brahir looked~~   brother

~~Up at the~~ , holding the bull's horn in one hand the knife in the

other looked up at the President's box . Handkerchiefs were waving

all over the bull ring . The President looked down from the box

and waved his handkerchief . The brother cut the notched black ear

from the dead bull and trotted over with it to Romero . The bull lay

heavy and black on the sand ,his tongue out . ~~People~~ were running   Boys

toward him from all parts of the Arena , making a little circle

around him . ~~People~~ They were starting to dance around the bull .

~~The man and the brother was wiping the bloody muleta~~

Romero took the ear from his brother and held it up

toward the President. The President bowed and Romero ,running to get

ahead of the crowd came toward us . He leaned up against the barrera

and gave the ear to Brett . He nodded his head and smiled . The crowd

In this revised version of the killing of the bull, Hemingway focused closely on
a series of particular moments (198-4-154).

As in the earlier description of Romero's first *quite,* the movement in the revision—which was toward a more exact description—led to shorter sentences (though the sentences in this descriptive passage are not so short as in the presentation of the earlier action) and attention to shorter units of time. And the action is not always so smoothly presented. In the first draft the matador, "having been one with the bull is then alone, the bull having broken the figure himself because the man has planned it so" (194-6-19). In the published version, the action does not end smoothly: "Romero lurched clear to the left" (*SAR,* p. 220). Again we are reminded of the immediate reality of what Hemingway is describing: a swordsman who plans the bull's action so as to let the bull break the unified figure that the two contestants form is very different from a man who, despite all his masterful planning, lurches clear of the bull. The method of presentaton has also been altered radically. Instead of a narrator who interprets the matador's planning, we have a narrator who carefully observes the action at hand and then reports in great detail. The narrator's expertise is no longer shown in interpretation, save for one carefully inserted judgment which alerts the reader to what is to follow: "He killed not as he had been forced to by the last bull, but as he wanted to" (198-4-154). Instead, Jake's expertise as an aficionado and observer of the bullfight is shown in his choice of what Hemingway earlier called "these special moments that novelists build their whole structures on" (194-1-9).

Having achieved an effective description of the climactic moment of the bullfight, Hemingway then faced the difficulty of leading his reader back away from that highly charged moment, a difficulty that led to his doing a good deal of additional revision in his description both of the *coup de grâce* administered to the bull and of the cutting of an ear as a trophy for Romero's performance. In describing these two actions, Hemingway reversed the approaches to revision that I have mentioned in earlier examples. He did not pare away his description to an irreducible minimum or eliminate whole sections of narration. Nor did he fine tune his description within the same framework of word length, as in the description of Jake and the waiter in the Pamplona café. Instead, he followed an approach similar to the one seen near the end of the café section, when he worked to add detail to the description of Vicente Girones's coffin being borne to the railway station.

As in the café section, after the presentation of Jake's conversation with the waiter, in the description of the bullfight the high point has been passed, and Hemingway is concerned with bringing his readers down, leading smoothly away from a moment of great intensity. He must provide a proper frame for the special moment in which Romero's bravery and skill are most clearly seen. In revising, Hemingway essentially doubled in length the description of the aftermath of the bullfight. His first-draft description of the aftermath is sketchily generalized:

He- *The bull* went to *down on* his knees and the puntillero Guerritas older brother *leaned forward* behind him and drove a short knife into his *the bull's* neck just at the base of the horns. The bull went over, twitching and

76

rigid. Guerrita's brother looked up at the President. All the handkerchiefs were waving ~~now~~. The President waved his and the brother leaning over cut the notched black ear from the dead bull and trotted over with it to Guerrita. Guerrita held it up toward the President. The President bowed and Guerrita, running to get ahead of the crowd came toward us. He leaned up against the barrera and gave the ear to Duff. [194-6-19; additions to the notebook are italicized]

This quoted section of Hemingway's first-draft description contains about 110 words; by the time final revisions had been completed, the comparable section of *The Sun Also Rises* had been expanded to about twice as many words. From eight sentences, the section had been expanded to thirteen, and a great deal of new detail—and some new information—had been added.

The first-draft version is not without detail: the bull goes over, "twitching and rigid"; Guerrita's brother does not cut merely an ear, but "the notched black ear." Guerrita's brother has not only stabbed the bull in the neck, but "just at the base of the horns." In making revisions, Hemingway had added layers of detail, slowing the tempo of presentation again and again by offering new information. Particularly, the tempo of the description of the death of the bull was slowed, almost to a painful extent. At the end of the new, substituted description of Romero's killing of the bull, Hemingway added "and it was over." What is over is not just the entire action of the bullfight but also Romero's active part in the killing of the bull. The focus shifts suddenly from Romero to the last moments of the bull. In the first-draft version, Hemingway had described the death fairly compactly, in two sentences that depicted the bull's fall to his knees, the *coup de grâce* delivered by the brother, and the final fall of the bull. In the revision, Hemingway chose to draw out his description, producing a more realistic and graphically described account of the bull's death and then adding additional detail, after the bull's death, in which his carcass still dominates the bullring:

The bull hesitated *swung from side to side and* then went down on his knees and Romero's older brother leaned forward behind him and drove a short knife into the bull's neck at the base of the horns. The first time he missed. He drove the knife in again and the bull went over, twitching and rigid. Romero's brother, holding the bull's horn in one hand the knife in the other looked up at the President's box. Handkerchiefs were waving all over the bull ring. The President looked down from the box and waved his handkerchief. The brother cut the notched black ear from the dead bull and trotted over with it to Romero. The bull lay heavy and black on the sand, his tongue out. Boys were running toward him from all parts of the Arena, making a little circle around him. They were starting to dance around the bull.

Romero took the ear from his brother and held it up toward the President. The President bowed and Romero, running to get ahead of the crowd came toward us. He leaned up against the barrera and gave the ear to Brett. [198-4-154; the italicized phrase was inked in on the typescript]

A moment in the bullring at Pamplona, 1925. Compare this picture to
Hemingway's description of the death of Romero's second bull.

The focus on the drawn-out death of the bull and the dominating presence of his
black carcass—the first focus of attention even for the boys who've jumped into the
ring—serves not only to lead away from the moment when the matador and the bull
are one but also to emphasize Romero's achievement. The carcass of the bull is
"heavy and black," a monolithic presence in the ring even after his death. In the
drawn-out description of his death (which incorporates another one of those few
handwritten additions to the typescript second draft, italicized above) Hemingway
created a terrible inertia. Even after Romero's masterful sword stroke, which
makes the death of the bull inevitable, that death is described in eight steps—the bull
will not die easily: (1) The bull tries to move forward; (2) his legs begin to give; (3)
he swings from side to side; (4) he hestitates; (5) he goes down on his knees; (6) he
takes the first stroke of the *coup de grâce;* (7) he takes the second knife stroke; and
(8) he falls, "twitching and rigid," finally dead. Carefully, step by step,
Hemingway's expert narrator has moved to the background and has allowed us to
see the bull's death as a process: this results in a wonder—namely, that a man, even
a Romero, could prevail against the brute vitality of such a beast. And the crowd's
celebration of Romero's achievement rightly focuses first on the vanquished bull
and then on the matador.

    In his description of the bullfight, Hemingway moved from Jake's explana-
tions, which are necessary for the reader's complete understanding of the action,

toward a direct presentation of moments that are significant because they exemplify the courage and controlled artistry that a man may aspire to and reach. None of the conventional "literary signs" that Hemingway inveighed against early in the first draft have been left to detract from those significant moments. Finally, the reader must decide on their meaning and importance—"You have to figure them out by yourself" (194-1-9).

Hemingway has carefully led his readers to this the climactic action of the novel, pointing the way in Jake's explanation of the bullfight and in his comments on the value of the work of the other matadors, as well as in earlier sections such as the description of the running of the bulls through the streets of Pamplona and the death of the aficionado Vicente Girones. The building to the climax has begun even as early as the first-draft version of Jake's comment to a world-weary Robert Cohn, which eventually appears as part of published chapter 2: " 'Nobody ever lives their life all the way up,' I said, 'except bull fighters' "(194-1-22).

THE FOURTH SCENE: JAKE ALONE
AND WITH BRETT (BOOK III)

Some of Hemingway's most extensive efforts at revision of *The Sun Also Rises* occur in the final chapter, which stands as Book III in the published novel. In the twenty-one pages of that section, Hemingway led away from the climactic events of the fiesta as Jake seeks a peaceful return to a less frenetic existence, then answers Brett's telegram and goes to retrieve her from Madrid.

As Hemingway worked toward a resolution of the action and thought of the entire novel, he returned to the extensive working out on paper of the themes and movements of the novel as they are reflected in the thoughts of Jake Barnes. But by this point in the process of composition, there seems to be much less confusion about the identity of the narrators: for example, we do not need to wonder, as we did early in the first draft, whether the narrative voice is that of Jake Barnes or the unfiltered, direct voice of Ernest Hemingway. Here, though the narrator of the first draft works out problems at great length, he does so in what is very clearly the voice of Jake Barnes. There are no confusions about the identity of the narrator such as occur in the early description of the funeral of Ernest/Jake's namesake uncle. While the musings of the narrator become obtrusive in their repetition, the repetitions that do occur are wholly believable as the obsessively recurring thoughts of a disturbed Jake Barnes.

That Hemingway eventually chose to relegate those musings to the submerged seven-eighths of his narrative iceberg reflects their failure to function as compelling narration; it does not present a problem of narrative voice. That is, in the deleted sections it is clearly Jake who is speaking; but he is not really giving us any information that is not already available in the chapter. He is not offering us new insights into what has occurred earlier in the book. And finally, having carefully worked out Jake's state of mind, Hemingway not only chose to omit most of his musings, concentrating on those experiences in which Jake seeks to reorder and compose himself; he also concentrated, not on Jake's *statements* about his reactions to the aftermath of the fiesta, but instead on the reactions themselves.

Appropriately, Jake's musings do not begin until after he has parted from Bill Gorton and Mike Campbell and installed himself overnight in a Bayonne hotel room. Jake sits and thinks that the next day he will leave Bayonne to go back into Spain to the seaside at San Sebastián:

> I wished I had gone up to Paris with Bill except that would have meant more fiesta-ing in Paris and I was through with Fiestas. It would be quiet in San Sebastian. The season did not open until August and I could get a good hotel room and read and swim. It was a splendid place to swim. You could lie on the beach and soak in the sun and get straightened around inside again. Maybe I would feel like writing. San Sebastian was a good place. There were wonderful trees along the promenade above the beach and there were good looking children sent down with their nurses before the season opened. In the evening there would be band concerts under the trees across from the Cafe Marinas. There was a nice old port. It would be quiet and solid and restful. [194-6-31]

Jake's pleasure in the thought of San Sebastián is clearly expressed, as it is clearly expressed in the published version of this passage. And in both versions, the descriptions of San Sebastián are pleasant, underlining Jake's judgments. Yet here in the first draft, those judgments are far more explicit than they would be after revision. Even in the published version, Jake idealizes San Sebastián, with its quiet, good hotel rooms, "fine beach," and "wonderful trees" (*SAR,* p. 232). But the first draft's emphases on quiet, restfulness, and getting "straightened around inside again" become submerged, though they are still clearly present by implication, and the reference to writing, perhaps the writing of *The Sun Also Rises,* is also dropped. (While composing this section Hemingway was in Paris; although he had earlier worked on the second notebook of the first draft while in San Sebastián, on 8 and 9 August 1925.)

While the first-draft version offers an effective essay on Jake's need for quiet, Hemingway's revisions made Jake less self-consciously wounded:

> I wished I had gone up to Paris with Bill, except that Paris would have meant more fiesta-ing. I was through with fiestas for a while. It would be quiet in San Sebastian. The season does not open there until August. I could get a good hotel room and read and swim. There was a fine beach there. There were wonderful trees along the promenade above the beach, and there were many children sent down with their nurses before the season opened. In the evening there would be band concerts under the trees across from the Café Marinas. I could sit in the Marinas and listen. [*SAR,* p. 232]

The Jake of the published version is more realistic, and he seems to be in better control of his emotions, though he is still not completely happy. Though he chooses not to continue "fiesta-ing" in Paris, he is not rejecting the idea of the fiesta completely, as in the first draft. Instead, he knows that he is through with fiestas only "for a while." He does not dwell obsessively on "getting straightened around," but instead takes a simple, pure pleasure in the thought of the "fine beach." As in the first draft, the trees along the promenade are "wonderful" in Jake's reflections, but Hemingway again interjects a more healthy realism into Jake's thoughts of the children sent down to the seashore; they are no longer described as "good looking," but more accurately become "many children."

Finally, Jake no longer directly states that San Sebastián will be "quiet and solid and restful." Instead, his thoughts of rest are presented in terms of the activities he plans: "In the evening there would be band concerts under the trees across from the Café Marinas. I could sit in the Marinas and listen" (*SAR*, p. 232). That final sentence, which comes at the end of the paragraph of contemplation, lingers delicately in the imagination, evoking an image "quiet and solid and restful" (194-6-31). Jake's desire for peace is never more clearly expressed than in his desire to sit in the café and listen.

Throughout this final chapter, Hemingway worked to set France in opposition to Spain, as the France of early Book I is set in opposition to Spain, where the novel's main action occurs. After meditating about what will happen in San Sebastián, Jake goes to dinner and analyzes the difference between French and Spanish meals (French meals seem "carefully apportioned" in comparison to those of Spain). He reflects that his French waiter's apparent friendship is designed to increase the size of his tip ("No one makes things complicated by becoming your friend" [194-6-32]; in revision, in the notebook, this judgment became: "No one makes things complicated by becoming your friend for any obscure reason" [194-6-32]).

Again and again, Hemingway continued to amend Jake's judgments, making him less a conscious commentator and more a man who is recording immediate experience. Thus, in his first-draft discussion of the French waiter's love of money, Jake carefully emphasizes the contradiction between the apparently easy values that the waiter represents and the real values that Jake espouses, values we've earlier seen represented by the Spanish waiter, who talks freely with Jake, or by a man like Romero: "It *seemed* comfortable to be in a country [France] where it is so simple to make people happy" (194-6-32; my italics). In making revisions, Hemingway submerged the irony of that *seemed,* substituting a more direct and less conspicuously ironic phrasing: "It felt comfortable" (*SAR*, p. 233).

At the bottom of the same page of *The Sun Also Rises,* Jake again records his feelings directly as he reenters Spain:

> At Irun we had to change trains and show passports. I hated to leave France. Life was so simple in France. I felt I was a fool to be going back

into Spain. In Spain you could not tell about anything. I felt like a fool to be going back into it, but I stood in line with my passport. [*SAR,* p. 233]

Here again the emphasis is on Jake's direct impressions and feelings; he does not analyze, but records directly: he feels like a fool. But behind this direct presentation of Jake's emotion stands an earlier analysis in which Hemingway presented Jake's rational working out of his emotions. The notebook first-draft version is:

> At Irun we had to change trains and show pass ports. I hated to leave France. Life was so simple in France. Never in France have I had any trouble nor have I had any adventures. In Spain you could not tell about anything. ~~Spain was another country~~. I felt I was a fool to be going back into it. . . . [194-6-33]

Here the difference between France and Spain is clearly stated: Jake gives us the reasons for his feeling a fool and simultaneously underlines the novel's France/Spain split in values.

But in a comparison of France and Spain, Jake Barnes, the expert commentator, is not so necessary as in the earlier description of the bullfight. The bullfight was new territory to the reader; an expert guide was required to enable the reader to understand the meaning of what was occurring in the arena. But in this final chapter, as Hemingway winds his story to a close, such an expert commentator is not needed—the France/Spain split in values has been implicit throughout the entire novel. And Hemingway has returned his focus to Jake, the confused and unhappy man; whereas in the bullfight scene he focused on Romero through Jake's clear-seeing eyes.

We have already seen that the Spain of the novel is a more authentic country than France; Spain is "another country" where trouble and adventures are all too possible. But in the first-draft version, Jake continues to belabor the point in a passage describing his first meal since returning to Spain:

> It was pleasant to have ~~too much~~ a great amount of food served again. You did not have to eat it and it was nice not to have that measured French feeling. There was only an old man in the dining room. He was eating a big lunch over against the window. He talked to his waitress when she brought him dishes and she seemed to be amused. I had Borrow's Bible in Spain with me and read through the meal *and drank a bottle of Alta Navarra.* [194-6-34; italicized words added in revision]

The mood of the café, with the old man talking to the waitress, is far different from the mood of the French café, at least in Jake's mind. The peace of the café is not unlike that found late at night in the Spanish café frequented by another old man, the old man of "A Clean, Well-Lighted Place." And Jake seems to be facing a nothingness similar to that faced by the old man of the 1933 story—a *nada* that is defined in the first draft by Jake's compulsively repeated discussions of his mental state while in San Sebastián. And the café in San Sebastián is similarly a focus for order and sanity. In another first-draft segment, which was later deleted, Jake sits on the terrace of the Café Marinas, listening to the orchestra that he earlier imagined, again dwelling obsessively on the therapeutic value of San Sebastián:

> San Sebastian was a good place. It was a good place to get all straightened inside again. I had a lot of books, a Turgenieff, two Mrs. Belloc-Lowndes, the Bible in Spain, I could get Tauchnitz if I wanted them. It would be fun to swim, to get up late, to eat good meals and to read. Then I could go back to Paris and get to work again. Paris would be nice and it would be fun to eat out at the ~~Park~~ Parc Montsouris and at the Quatre Seigents de la Rochelle again. It was always fun to get back to Paris.
> After the concert ~~stopped in~~ *was over inside* the café I paid for my drink and walked out to the old harbour, Then I walked all the way around the harbour, along the promenade and way beyond and then turned back and walked into the town and to the hotel to get supper. I was very hungry. It was beginning to get dark as I came away from the harbor and through the streets to the hotel. [194-6-36; addition italicized]

Again, in revising, Hemingway noted Jake's obsessive refrain, moving the emphasis from his disordered thoughts to the presentation of the ordered world around him. By doing so, Hemingway avoided the jarring juxtaposition of Jake's racing thoughts, on the one hand, with the surrounding quiet images on the other. In revising, he shortened the above quoted section into a description in which Jake no longer protests too much about what he would do to get straightened around, but instead submerges himself in present events, calming and ordered:

> I sat in front of the Marinas for a long time and read and watched the people, and listened to the music.
> Later when it began to get dark, I walked around the harbor and out along the promenade, and finally back to the hotel for supper. [*SAR*, 235]

Jake has come to rest, just as he hoped he would.

Even in San Sebastián, however, Jake's rest will be broken—eventually by Brett's telegram from Madrid, but first by the intrusion of the "French" values that he had hoped to escape, represented by the arrival of a group of racing bicycle riders. In the first-draft version, the French and Spanish riders are specifically set in opposition to each other: "The french riders did not think much of the competition given them by the spaniards" (194-6-37). The team's chauvinistic manager, much as in the final published version, pontificates on the sport and on France:

> The Tour de France was the greatest sporting event in the world. All spring and summer and fall he spent on the roads with the riders. It had made him know France. That is a thing few people know. It was a very ~~strange country. He knew~~ beautiful country. A very rich country. The number of motor cars now that followed the racers from town to town on the great circuit. It was a rich country and more *sportif* every year. It

would be the most *sportif* country in the world. It was road racing did it, road racing and football. He knew France—*La France Sportif.* He knew road racing. After all though it wasnt so bad to be back in Paris. Not so bad. There is only one Paris. Paris is the town the most *sportif* in the world. [194-6-38; Hemingway's italics]

Jake's decision to avoid the excitement of fiestas and the corruption of France's money-centered culture is emphasized, in all drafts, by his decision to sleep in rather than to accept the manager's invitation to attend the departure of the tour. Jake's rejection of bicycle racing seems also to represent a significant deviation from Hemingway's opinions on the sport. In *A Moveable Feast* he later wrote, "I have started many stories about bicycle racing but have never written one that is as good as the races are both on the indoor and outdoor tracks and on the roads" (*MF,* p. 64). The point is worth making, for this difference serves to suggest what I have maintained elsewhere: namely, that even in the first draft of *The Sun Also Rises,* Hemingway carefully distanced himself from his fictional narrator; and this distancing is one thing that makes the novel much more than a simple journalistic recounting of events. And his expressed affection for bicycle racing has been subordinated to the place of the sport within the novel's scheme of meaning.

The final intrusion on Jake's holiday in San Sebastián cannot be so easily ignored as can the departure of the French cyclists. A telegram arrives from Madrid; another is forwarded from Pamplona: "COULD YOU COME HOTEL MONTANA/AM RATHER IN TROUBLE DUFF" (194-6-40). In the first draft, Jake's reaction is at once bitter and resigned:

> Well that meant San Sebastian all shot to hell. I suppose, vaguely, I had expected something of the sort. Oh well it was the price one paid for knowing the aristocracy. Someone had to pay for the aristocracy. I was being very hard headed and disgusted about it. I saw the concierge standing inside the doorway.
> "Bring me a telegraph form, please," I said.
> He brought it with a pen and ink. I ~~waved~~ took out my fountain pen and printed
>
>
>
> LADY ~~ANthony~~ Ashley
> HOTEL MONTANA
> MADRID
> ARRIVING SUD EXPRESS TOMORROW
>
>
> then I stopped. That handled the matter. There was nothing else to say. ~~I put the~~ What else was there to say? I printed LOVE JAKE and handed the concierge the wire. There I was, doing it again. Why not let it alone. I knew there was not any use trying to let it alone. I felt perfectly hard about it. I had certainly acted like anything but a man. Send a girl off with one man. Introduce her to another to go off with him. Now go and bring her back. And sign the wire with love. [194-6-41]

In the first draft, Jake goes on at great length (about three and a half notebook pages) to discuss the aristocracy, which Braddocks has labeled the "good people." Jake and Brett have appropriated the term, ironically dubbing themselves "good people," though they might not exactly fit Braddocks's definition. (The term is most closely associated with the characters of Ford Madox Ford's 1915 masterpiece, *The Good Soldier: A Tale of Passion.*) Musing on his relationship with Duff, Jake simultaneously returns to a single example of the sort of discussion of reality in art which occurred early in the first draft. In this one discussion, Hemingway seems to speak more directly than elsewhere in the chapter; the ideas of the real and of the fictional narrators become difficult to sort out until, at the end of the discussion, Jake's wound reappears in his musings, helping to make the division clearer.

> In [Braddocks's novels] there was always a great deal of passion but it took sometimes ~~three~~ two and three volumes for anyone to sleep with anyone else. In actual life it seemed there was a great deal of sleeping about among good people ~~and when there was any actual passion nobody believed in it~~ much more sleeping about than passion. . . . Who knew anything about anybody? You didn't know a woman because you slept with her any more than you knew a horse because you'd ridden him once. . . . Besides you learned a lot about a woman by not sleeping with her. I ought to be glad I was the way I was. Oh yes very glad. Glad as hell. Nothing like recognizing your advantages. I went in to lunch. [194-6-42 and 43]

Jake discusses his emotional turmoil quite plainly in the above two quotations: the discussion of his doubts about his own manhood is generated as he analyzes his motives for signing the wire "with love." And his extremely disturbed state is further demonstrated by the three-and-a-half-page digression on the "good people." His view of the relationships between emotion, passion, and sex as a physical act similarly seems to be generated out of Jake's unhappiness. That view—namely, that there is more sleeping about than actual passion and that knowing a woman is not the same as sleeping with her—seems to be part of a mature and accurate view of the world. But the tone of that view's discussion ("You didn't know a woman because you slept with her any more than you knew a horse because you'd ridden him once") hardly seems mature; certainly it is not objective. Similarly, the use of Braddocks/Ford's novels as targets helps to initiate the discussion of passion, but really is not organic to the discussion. Furthermore, the treatment of the books is both perfunctory and out of character for Jake, a journalist who knows Braddocks. Finally, the extreme length of the analysis interferes with the movement of the novel to its close.

In making revisions, Hemingway projected a Jake Barnes who was more in character and more controlled and mature, though he was still not without some bitterness. Hemingway cut the entire three and one-half pages of digression on "good people" and passion, thus producing a far smoother flow, with all the above material reduced to:

Well, that meant San Sebastian all shot to hell. I suppose, vaguely, I had expected something of the sort. I saw the concierge standing in the doorway.

"Bring me a telegram form, please."

He brought it and I took out my fountain-pen and printed:

LADY ASHLEY HOTEL MONTANA MADRID
ARRIVING SUD EXPRESS TOMORROW LOVE
JAKE.

That seemed to handle it. That was it. Send a girl off with one man. Introduce her to another to go off with him. Now go and bring her back. And sign the wire with love. That was it all right I went in to lunch. [*SAR*, p. 239]

In one further suggestion of Jake's emotional turmoil, Hemingway compensated for the pages of cut material with one detail that achieved a similar effect. In the rough-draft version of the first sentence after Jake has gone in to lunch, Jake sleeps well as he travels to Madrid on the Sud Express; but in the published version, he "did not sleep much that night on the Sud Express" (*SAR*, p. 239). As in so many other revisions, the effect of that tiny change is considerable; in that one sentence, Hemingway has done as much to suggest Jake's mental state as he did in the three and one-half pages of unrevised material. Thus Jake's anguished reflections have become part of the submerged seven-eighths. His sleeplessness suggests all that underlies it, which is invisible yet present. The early-draft explanations of Jake's mental state have been replaced by a much more direct presentation.

In succeeding sections, Hemingway continued to cut as he revised. In its final form, Jake's journey to Madrid is presented in one short descriptive passage in which Jake's feelings are set in opposition to the fact that he "did not give a damn" about the scenery (*SAR*, p. 239), while in the notebook draft the journey included a discussion of how it "kills something" to cover distance rapidly.

A good deal of extraneous explanation was deleted as Hemingway set his scenes. For example, whereas in the final version of the novel the Hotel Montana is quite adequately categorized by saying that it occupies the second story of a building and that its elevator cannot be made to work, in the early versions, Hemingway took great pains to explain: "The Montana was a pension. The English translation of a pension is boarding house. But it is not a boarding house. It is a cheap hotel where you have to take your meals" (194-6-44). Hemingway cut this explanation early, crossing it out in the notebook draft as part of his general streamlining revision of the entire chapter.

Also streamlined in revision were Jake's comic conversation with the woman who runs the pension and his succeeding meeting with Brett. Both of the initial versions of these two conversations run a good deal longer than the eventual published versions of them. As published, the two are subtly juxtaposed: the comic misunderstandings of Jake's impatient conversation with the hotel's manager serve to whet the reader's desire to get on to the upcoming confrontation between Jake and Brett; the inanity of the first conversation also stands in marked contrast to the sudden, unexpected level of mature understanding that Brett shows as she talks of her decision not to stay with Romero. But both of these functional juxtapositions seem to have been developed in revision. In the notebook draft, the conversation between Jake and the manager works as an end in itself rather than as a careful introductory transition to the second conversation. And the confrontation between Jake and Duff suffers the same problems of maudlin wordiness that marked their love scene in Book I.

Hemingway eliminated six lines of dialogue from Jake's conversation with the manager and more than two notebook pages of dialogue from Jake's conversation with Duff/Brett. The conversation between Jake and the manager is even less rational in its first-draft version than in the published one:

> "Muy buenos," I said. "Is there an Englishwoman here? I would like to see this English lady."
> "Muy buenos. Yes there is an English female English. Certainly you can see her if she wishes to see you."
> "She wishes to see me."
> "The chica will ask her."
> *"Is this female English a blood relation? of you?"
> *"She is the sister of my sister."
> *"Ah yes "Clearly. Then you are her uncle."
> "It is very hot."
> "It is very hot in summer in Madrid."
> "And how cold in winter."
> "Yes. It is very cold in winter." Including that I find the Madrid
> *"Including that I find Madrid muy bonita."
> *"If Madrid had the sea what a place."
> *"That would be bonita." [194-6-44 and 45; my asterisks mark
> lines that were subsequently deleted]

In this first-draft version, even the logical progression of the dialogue does not alternate regularly between Jake and the manager. And their conversation about the weather (introduced by Jake) becomes as absurd in its imagining of a seaside Madrid as does the manager's earlier attempt to identify Jake as a relative who might see Brett without any impropriety. The fractured logic of the exchange makes for appealingly light reading as Hemingway ridicules the use of language as a means of obfuscation rather than communication; but it had to be toned down in revision, leaving the major emphasis to fall on the much more important ensuing conversation between Jake and Brett.

Early versions of the latter conversation were a good deal longer. In the first-draft version, Brett often seems less sure of herself, less at peace with the decisions that she has made. In the pages that were cut from the notebook draft, her insecurity is plain, as in this selection:

"You hate me don't you."

"Just a little."

"It's all right," she said, "I deserve it."

"No you dont."

"Do you love me still?"

"I guess so."

"You don't love me any more. It's all right."

"I love you. But I try so damn hard not to." [194-6-46]

In the revision, these guilty discussions were cut, while Hemingway expanded Brett's discussion of her relationship with Romero. In the first draft, Duff/Brett is sure of her own power to keep Romero, even more sure than in Hemingway's revised version:

"You could have kept him." [Jake says]

"I should hope so. It isnt the sort of thing one does. I don't think I hurt him any." [194-6-46]

In the revised version, Brett is presented as less sure of why she has given up Romero: she simply follows her instincts, which have a good deal to do with concern for people other than herself:

"Why didn't you keep him?" [Jake asks]

"I don t know. It isn't the sort of thing one does. I don't think I hurt him any." [*SAR,* p. 241]

In the first-draft version, Brett explains her actions fairly freely, without Jake's questioning her; whereas in the final version, her story emerges in the give-and-take of a conversation. In the first draft:

"Oh hell," she said. "Let's not talk about it. Let's never talk about it."

"Only if there's anything you want to get off your chest."

"Oh no. It was rather a knock him being ashamed of me. He wanted me to grow my hair out. Me, with long hair. *Can you see it?* I'd look so like hell."

"That was funny."

"He said it would make me more womanly.** I'd look a fright."

"What was it about being in trouble?" [194-6-47]

In the revised version, Jake's continued comments elicit more information, and the effect is much less that of having Brett give a speech and much more a matter of having her unburden herself to Jake, whom she both respects and trusts:

"Oh, hell!" she said, "let's not talk about it. Let's never talk about it."

"All right."

"It was rather a knock his being ashamed of me. He was ashamed of me for a while, you know."

"No."

" You were probably damn good for him."

" He shouldn't be living with anyone . I realized that
right away ."

" No."

" Oh hell ," she said." Let's not talk about it . Let's never
talk about it ."

" All right ."

" It was rather a knock his being ashamed of me . He was
ashamed of me for a while you know . "

" No."

" Oh yes. They ragged him about me at the cafe I guess. He
wanted me to grow my hair out . Makexmexnorexwomanlynell Me , with
long hair . I'd look so like hell."
~~Ixkeexlyxxl~~
~~lxxkxexnexexxxgexnxxxx~~
      It's funny .

" He said it would make me more womanly . I'd look a
fright ."

" What happened ?"

" Oh he got over that . ~~Wasn't~~ He ashamed of me long . "

" What was it about being in trouble ?"

" I didn't know whether I could make him go and
I didn't have a sou to go away and leave him . He tried to give
me a lot of money you know . I told him I had scads of it . He knew
that was a lie . I couldn't take his money you know ."

" No."

" Oh let's not talk about it . There were some funny things
though . ~~He learned his English being a waiter in Gibralter.~~ "
~~Do give me a cigarette.~~
I lit the cigarette
" ~~He learned his English~~ as a waiter in gib".

" He wanted to marry me finally ."

" Really ?"

A late typescript of the conversation in which Brett tells Jake why she gave up
Romero. This is one of the pages that Hemingway typed himself; notice his
characteristic spacing before many marks of punctuation (198-4-177).

"Oh, yes. They ragged him about me at the café, I guess. He wanted
me to grow my hair out. Me, with long hair. I'd look so like hell."
"It's funny."
"He said it would make me look more womanly. I'd look a fright."
"What happened?"
"Oh, he got over that. He wasn't ashamed of me long."
"What was it about being in trouble?" [*SAR*, p. 242]

Running through each version of the scene is Brett's comment, which is ironic
in the context of the discussion of her relationship with Romero, "Let's not talk
about it." Brett's revelations work against her stated desire not to discuss what has
happened. Jake stands far enough back to make the careful comments that will elicit
the facts of Brett's relationship with Romero, but he stands close enough to her
emotionally that she will respond to him.

Quite obviously, the Brett of this scene is far different from the aloof,
controlled Brett we see so often earlier in the novel. She has changed: Hemingway,
by inserting material to substitute for the two-plus pages that he deleted earlier in
the scene, had shown that change physically, as Brett first greets Jake and as he
holds her. In the published version, the embrace is presented this way:

"Darling!" Brett said.
I went over to the bed and put my arms around her. She kissed me,
and while she kissed me I could feel she was thinking of something else.
She was trembling in my arms. She felt very small. [*SAR*, p. 241]

The clues to the changes in Brett—namely, that she was "thinking of something
else" and that she "felt very small"—stand in contrast to earlier presentations of
her character. All too often earlier, she thought of nothing or was "blind" or
drunk. And she never seemed physically small: she was assured in the face she
presented to the world, a strong woman. In the first draft, Hemingway had made
the contrast even more obvious in a line that he deleted before publication, one of
those "literary signs" that Hemingway was at pains to submerge. This is the first
version:

She was thinking of something else. I could feel her heart beating
under my hand. She was trembling too a little. She felt so small. I had
always thought of us as about the same size. [194-6-46]

Brett's façade has not proved adequate to shield her from an authentic involvement
with Romero; but in spite of the depth of that involvement, she has given him up.

Although the final book of *The Sun Also Rises* consists of just one chapter, the
division into books did not exist until the typescript second draft. As Hemingway
worked over the notebook version, he considered splitting that single chapter into
two, and he actually wrote in a division, "Chapter XXII," just at the end of the
scene in which Brett explains why she has left Romero. The experimental chapter
division comes just before Jake and Brett leave the Hotel Montana; the position of

emphasis at the end of the chapter would thus have been held by Brett's last anguished restatement of her reason for leaving Romero and the extent of her loss:

> She would not look up. I stroked her hair. I could feel her shaking.
> "I won't be one of those bitches," she said. "But oh Jake. Please lets never never talk about it." [194-6-48]

Hemingway rewrote an earlier passage thus:

> "No."
> "In Paris you can't tell whether a boys with his wife or his mother."
> "I know."
> "I'm not going to be that way. I'm damned if I am. I feel rather good you know. I feel rather set up."
> "Dear Duff."
> Chapter XXII
> We left the Hotel Montana. [194-6-48]

Then he circled the passage ending with "Dear Duff" and moved it up to just before "I put my arms around her."

Interpretations of *The Sun Also Rises* that consider Brett solely as an unchanging character, an unthinking bitch-goddess, must founder on the second confrontation between Jake and Brett. As the two leave the Hotel Montana—they find that there was no *financial* reason for Jake to rescue Brett, since Romero has behaved as honorably in leaving Brett as she behaved in making him go: Romero has paid her bill. In "Chapter XXII" of the intermediate draft (the last four-plus pages of the novel as it was finally published), Hemingway revised a good deal. Yet here the essential tone of his first draft carried clearly through into the ending of the published novel.

The use of a separate chapter might have contributed to a clearer understanding of the change that had taken place in Brett and the change that had occurred in the relationship between Jake and Brett by separating the two kinds of actions with the chapter break. The chapter division was not inserted cursorily and then immediately dropped; it carried through from its insertion in the notebook first draft into the typescript versions of the novel; but it is absent from the published text. It is not extremely difficult to discern why. A reasonable conjecture might involve the relative lengths of the two chapters that would thus have made up Book III—the first being fairly long at seventeen pages; the second being very short at about four. Most important, the short final chapter, it should be reemphasized, became a part of a larger ending unit, as Hemingway introduced the book divisions into the novel in its typescript version, much as he later divided *A Farewell to Arms* into five books at an intermediate stage of its composition (see Reynolds, p. 53).

In the final few pages of the notebook draft, Duff/Brett has moved from dependence on Jake to a position of equality. As she leaves the Hotel Montana, she leaves behind the what-might-have-been of her relationship with Romero and moves into a new, a mutually tolerant and understanding, relationship with Jake. From the stormy emotionalism of the scene in the Montana, the two move to a calm scene which takes its tone from Jake's comment "It's wonderful what a wonderful gentility there is in the bar of a big hotel" (194-6-49). The two find comfort in each other's company and in their pleasant surroundings, though Jake continues to protest just a little too much: "Bartenders have always been wonderful" (194-6-49). In revising this final section, Hemingway generally worked for the exact expression of an effect that was already present in the first draft. Thus, in Jake's two lines, Hemingway's revisions worked to reduce his intrusive rather than functional insistence on *wonderful*: "It's *funny* what a wonderful gentility you get in the bar of a big hotel. . . . Bartenders have always been *fine*" (198-4-180; my italics).

Yet even in a section that operates this smoothly, Hemingway found it necessary to make one major substitution of material, as Jake and Brett finish their meal in Botin's. Here, as in the San Sebastián section earlier in Book III, Jake is perhaps a little too self-aware in the first draft, a little too conscious of why he does what he does, in compensation for the things he cannot do:

> "It's funny how many things you can find comfort in." [Jake says]
> "Yes. You like to eat dont you?" Duff said.
> "Yes, I like to eat and I like to drink and I like to lead a quiet life and I like to read books."
> "You're a little drunk," Duff said. "What else do you like?"
> "Oh I like horse races and I like bull fights and I like to fish and I like to eat and drink."
> "You said that."
> "I know it."
> "I like to sail," Duff said.
> "Yes," I said. "I like to sail too."
> "Sailing's rather wonderful," Duff said. [194-6-54]

Hemingway almost completely rewrote the exchange in the typescript draft, drawing the emphasis away from a direct statement and avoiding the list of activities that Jake finds comfort in. Jake simply says, twice, "I like to do a lot of things" (198-4-182). Instead, Hemingway emphasized Jake's mild escapism: Jake drinks three bottles of *rioja alta* and eats a big meal, and it is Brett who senses just what he is doing, rather than he who explains his own actions:

> "How do you feel, Jake?" Brett asked. "My God! what a meal you've eaten."
> "I feel fine. Do you want a dessert?"
> "Lord, no."
> Brett was smoking.
> "You like to eat, don't you" she said.
> "Yes," I said. "I like to do a lot of things."
> "What do you like to do?"
> "Oh," I said. "I like to do a lot of things. Don't you want a dessert."
> "You asked me that once," Brett said. [*SAR*, p. 246]

The first-draft ending of the novel. Notice that Hemingway was already trying alternative phrasings for the last line, as he worked for the precise effect he wanted (194-6-55).

184

where to drive and got in beside Brett . The driver started up the
street . I settled back . Brett moved close to me . We sat close
against each other . I put my arm around her and she rested
     comfortably .
against me/. It was very hot and bright and the houses looked
sharply white . We turned out onto the Gran Via .

          " Oh Jake ," Brett said. " We could have had such a
damned good time together ."

               Ahead was a mounted policeman in khaki directing traffic .
He raised his baton and whistled . The car slowed suddenly pressing
Brett against me .

          " Yes ," I said." Isn't it pretty to think so."

                    THE END

In the revised version of the book's ending, Hemingway altered the pacing and
tone of the scene (198-4-184).

Continually throughout this section, along with this large substitution of
material, Hemingway worked to convey the mutual comforting and tolerance of the
two, even as Jake becomes drunk and a little self-pitying. Thus, instead of Brett
putting "her hand on my thigh under the table" (194-6-54), she "put her hand on
my arm" (*SAR*, p. 246). Intead of "I put my arm around her and she rested her
body against me" (194-6-55), we have "she rested against me comfortably" (*SAR*,
p. 247).

Hemingway also reworked his last few lines, striving for the precisely
appropriate effect. The first draft ends with:

> "Oh Jake," Duff said. "We could have had such a damned good
> time together."
> Ahead was a mounted policeman in Khaki. T directing traffic. The
> car slowed suddenly pressing Duff closer against me.
> "Yes," I said. "It's nice as hell to think so."
> *The End.*
>   Paris—Sept. 21—1925 [194-6-55]

Here, even as the two skirt about the most difficult aspects of their relationship,
Hemingway was working in careful detail, using the appearance of the mounted
policeman and the slowing cab to lend verisimilitude and to slow the reader, so that

Duff's question and Jake's answer will not blend too quickly into each other. But even here the precise expression had not been achieved: Jake still seems petulant and aggrieved rather than comforted with his "It's nice as hell to think so."

Reworking the first draft later, in a black ink that contrasts with the blue ink of the first draft of the text in this notebook, Hemingway wrote a second version at the bottom of the page: "Isn't it nice to think so" (194-6-55)—a wearier, yet more peaceful, expression.

In his typescript version, Hemingway introduced an explanation of why the cab slowed, which simultaneously served to separate the two lines of dialogue even more: "Ahead was a mounted policeman in khaki directing traffic. *He raised his baton and whistled*" (198-4-184; my italics). Hemingway also, of course, changed *Duff* to *Brett* and found an even more appropriate expression of Jake's realistic, weary, yet essentially healthy accommodation to the realities of his relationship with Brett. Also, Hemingway later eliminated the sound of the policeman's whistle, leaving a silent pause between Brett's statement and Jake's rhetorical question:

"Oh, Jake," Brett said, "we could have had such a damned good time together."

Ahead was a mounted policeman in khaki directing traffic. He raised his baton. The car slowed suddenly pressing Brett against me.

"Yes," I said. "Isn't it pretty to think so?"

THE END [*SAR*, p. 247]

6

Late Revisions:
Hemingway and Fitzgerald

While most of the revisions of *The Sun Also Rises* took place either on the pages of the notebook first draft or in the recasting of that draft into typescript form, one major revision occurred very late in the composition of the novel—after it had been accepted by Scribner's and set in galley proofs. And unlike the other revisions, which seem to have been painstakingly worked out by Hemingway himself, this revision was strongly influenced by an outside reader—F. Scott Fitzgerald.

Hemingway had refused to let Fitzgerald see the manuscript first draft of the novel until it had been revised into final form:

> I explained to him that it would mean nothing until I had gone over it and rewritten it and that I did not want to discuss it or show it to anyone first. . . .
> . . . Scott did not see it until after the completed rewritten and cut manuscript had been sent to Scribners at the end of April. I remembered joking with him about it and him being worried and anxious to help as always once a thing was done. But I did not want his help while I was rewriting. [*MF*, pp. 184–85]

Hemingway's contention that the manuscript "would mean nothing" until it had been revised makes sense, both in terms of his possible desire for his work to appear at its best before Fitzgerald, who had just that same year published a masterwork, the splendidly controlled *The Great Gatsby,* and also in terms of *The Sun Also Rises'* own developing structure of meaning and style. The relatively uncontrolled first draft of the novel is not an accurate indication of Hemingway's capabilities in prose fiction, nor is it more than a rough indication of the structure of meaning of the final version.

However, Hemingway's statement that Fitzgerald did not see the novel until after the "rewritten and cut" manuscript had been sent to the publisher led to the long-held conclusion that Hemingway was claiming that Fitzgerald had not had any direct influence on the shape of the final novel. Such was not quite the case. Instead, according to Philip Young and Charles Mann, the compilers of the 1969 inventory of the Hemingway papers which were later collected in the Kennedy Library, Fitzgerald read a carbon copy of the final draft after that draft had indeed been sent off to Scribner's but before Hemingway had finished checking the novel in galley proofs. They based their conclusion upon a ten-page critique in Fitzgerald's handwriting, which was found folded into one of the notebooks of the first draft. In the scrawled letter to Hemingway, Fitzgerald carefully argued for the deletion of a good deal of the novel's beginning, all the way through the first two chapters that were eventually published. Fitzgerald suggested that Hemingway should begin with Jake's meeting the prostitute Georgette, at the beginning of the published chapter 3.

Carefully referring by page numbers and quoted passages to elements that he considered to be marked by "condescending casualness," Fitzgerald makes a case for deletion of the early material, reminding Hemingway that "the fact that people have committed themselves to you will make them watch you like a cat. & if they don't like it creap [*sic*] away like one." Fitzgerald is careful not to attack Hemingway's achievements in *The Sun Also Rises;* instead he phrases his more general comments in a manner that is likely to appeal to Hemingway's commitment to craftsmanlike work: "You can't play with people's attention—a good man who has the power of arresting attention at will must be especially careful." As conclusive evidence that Fitzgerald did read the novel in carbon copy after the final version had been sent to the publisher, Young and Mann point to the letter's comment "Please see what you can do about it in the proofs."

The first three galley proof sheets of *The Sun Also Rises* were discovered among the other Hemingway papers. A careful examination of the three galley proofs and Fitzgerald's letter (which were held in different locations when Young and Mann compiled their inventory) as well as the typescript and carbon copies of the final draft of the novel confirms Young and Mann's conclusion and adds new information. Fitzgerald did read a carbon copy of the final draft of the novel, and he did suggest changes to Hemingway, which Hemingway eventually implemented in part by eliminating the first one and one-half chapters of the typescript draft, approximately thirty-five hundred words. While he eventually just began with the next sentence after the cut material, Hemingway first tried several devices to fill the place of the deleted material, including a new beginning, in which he discussed and explained that he had cut out such material as well as an introduction to the novel.

The tone of the material that he eventually deleted is reminiscent of Hemingway's first-draft working out of ideas, motivations, and character traits; it

THE SUN ALSO RISES

BOOK I

CHAPTER I

THIS is a novel about a lady. Her name is Lady Ashley and when the story begins she is living in Paris and it is Spring. That should be a good setting for a romantic but highly moral story. As every one knows, Paris is a very romantic place. Spring in Paris is a very happy and romantic time. Autumn in Paris, although very beautiful, might give a note of sadness or melancholy that we shall try to keep out of this story.

Lady Ashley was born Elizabeth Brett Murray. Her title came from her second husband. She had divorced one husband for something or other, mutual consent; not until after he had put one of those notices in the papers stating that after this date he would not be responsible for any debt, etc. He was a Scotchman and found Brett much too expensive, especially as she had only married him to get rid of him and to get away from home. At present she had a legal separation from her second husband, who had the title, because he was a dipsomaniac, he having learned it in the North Sea commanding a mine-sweeper, Brett said. When he had gotten to be a proper thoroughgoing dipsomaniac and found that Brett did not love him he tried to kill her, and between times slept on the floor and was never sober and had great spells of crying. Brett always declared that it had been one of the really great mistakes of her life to have married a sailor. She should have known better, she said, but she had sent the one man she had wanted to marry off to Mesopotamia so he would last

out the war, and he had died of some very unromantic form of dysentery and she certainly could not marry Jake Barnes, so when she had to marry she had married Lord Robert Ashley, who proceeded to become a dipsomaniac as before stated.

They had a son and Ashley would not divorce, and would not give grounds for divorce, but there was a separation and Brett went off with Mike Campbell to the Continent one afternoon, she having offered to at lunch because Mike was lonely and sick and very companionable, and, as she said, "obviously one of us." They arranged the whole business before the Folkestone-Boulogne train left London at 9,30 that night. Brett was always very proud of that. The speed with which they got passports and raised funds. They came to Paris on their way to the Riviera, and stayed the night in a hotel which had only one room free and that with a double bed. "We'd no idea of anything of that sort," Brett said. "Mike said we should go on and look up another hotel, but I said no, to stop where we were. What's the odds." That was how they happened to be living together.

Mike at that time was ill. It was all he had brought back with him from the two years he had spent in business in Spain, after he had left the army, except the beautifully engraved shares of the company which had absorbed all of the fifteen thousand pounds that had come to him from his father's estate. He was also an undischarged bankrupt, which is quite a serious thing in England, and had various habits that Brett felt sorry for, did not think a man should have, and cured by constant watchfulness and the exercise of her then very strong will.

Mike was a charming companion, one of the most charming. He was nice and he was weak and he had a certain very hard gentleness in him that could not be touched and that never disappeared until the liquor

The beginning of the first of three galleys that Hemingway cut from *The Sun Also Rises* at least partly in response to F. Scott Fitzgerald's criticisms (202a)

is essentially expository rather than dramatic. In his first chapter the narrator discusses two of the novel's main characters, Brett and Mike, at once giving information on their personal backgrounds and analyzing their personalities, particularly as those personalities are reflected in their life in bohemian Paris. The method of discussion is very similar to the one that Hemingway used in introducing the published version of the novel, in the description of Robert in chapter 1.

In the typescript, Jake begins his narration with a brief paragraph in which he sets the scene of the novel's first book:

> This is a novel about a lady. ~~She does not appear for about twenty pages. Originally the book started off with~~ Her name is Lady Ashley and when the story begins she is living in Paris and it is Spring. That should be a good setting for a romantic but highly moral story. As every one knows Paris is a very romantic place. Spring in Paris is a very happy and romantic time. Autumn in Paris, although very beautiful, might give a note of sadness or melancholy that we shall try to keep out of this story.
> [202d; the passage that is lined through was crossed out on the typewriter]

Fitzgerald singled out the remark on the "highly moral story" as his first example of the elements in the first chapter that give "a feeling of condescending *casuallness.*" The passage would probably convey this impression to most readers. Though such heavily ironic statements on romance and morality might have been read differently if they had been placed in the context of Jake's wound and his natural reactions to Mike's relationship with Brett, here no such context has been established, and the feeling that is evoked does not adequately characterize Jake's ambivalent state as an emotionally involved narrator who is struggling to maintain his objectivity.

This chapter contained a great deal of information about Brett and Mike, much of which is available elsewhere in the novel (though it is not necessarily accessible without more effort on the reader's part than would be required in this cut first chapter), but at least as much of which is not. In addition to factual background, here Jake/Hemingway makes available to the reader some judgments that are only implied elsewhere. In the novel as published, much less is given, and much more is left for the reader to discover in accordance with Hemingway's earlier comment "you have to figure [things] out by yourself" (194-1-9).

In the cut chapter 1, we learn that Brett has been married twice, has been divorced once, and is now living apart from her second husband, Lord Ashley, "a dipsomaniac, he having learned it in the North Sea commanding a mine-sweeper" (202a, galley 1). She has had a son by Ashley, but apparently has not really loved either of her husbands; the two men whom she has loved have not turned out well for her. The first had sat out World War I in one of its safer theaters, Mesopotamia, until "he had died of some very unromantic form of dysentery and she certainly could not marry Jake Barnes" (202a, galley 1). And so, instead, Brett had married her second husband, who had already become unbalanced as a result of his war service and who had become suicidal when he learned that she really did not love him.

Mike Campbell and his relationship with Brett are introduced in the context of Brett's previous unloving or unfulfilled relationships with men. Mike and Brett have become lovers by chance, while traveling from London to the Riviera. They have undertaken the trip on an impulse, with platonic intentions, but they find themselves, because of a lack of planning, in Paris at a hotel with only one vacant room, and Brett declines Mike's suggestion that they try another hotel.

Mike, as is made clear elsewhere in the novel, is bankrupt; Jake describes him as having nothing left from his business venture in Spain but the "beautifully engraved shares" of the failed company which has absorbed his £15,000 inheritance. Fitzgerald singled out the "beautifully engraved shares" as "(Beautifully engraved 1886 irony) All this is O.K. but so glib when its [sic] glib + so profuse." He generally objected to Hemingway's biographies of the characters, citing Hemingway's own expressed belief "in the superiority (the preferability) of the *imagined* to the *seen not to say to the merely recounted.*"

Among the information not included in *The Sun Also Rises* are at least two additional facts: (1) that Mike, during the time span of the novel, is very ill, though his exact illness remains unnamed; and (2) that Mike may have had homosexual tendencies, though this fact is only rather faintly implied: He "had various habits that Brett felt sorry for, did not think a man should have, and cured by constant watchfulness and the exercise of her then very strong will" (202a, galley 1).

The chapter ends with a fairly long analysis of Brett's and Mike's drinking, its roots in the boredom of a remittance man's existence, ever waiting for the arrival, always late, of Mike's weekly allowance from home, an allowance that he has already borrowed against in advance. Mike is described as being a very well behaved drunk until he becomes extremely drunk. Then he is like "a bone [which] is dissolved in vinegar to prove it has something or other in it and if it were a long enough bone and you had used enough vinegar, you could even tie it into a knot" (202a, galley 1): he is utterly changed by alcohol. This analysis, of course, gives information that is later dramatized as Mike actually becomes drunk. The discussion of Brett's drinking also gives information, for drinking leaves her almost exactly the same as when she is sober: "She was always clear run, generous, and her lines were always as clear" (202a, galley 1). But as is implied later in the novel, her characterization of herself as becoming "blind drunk" is essentially a literal description: though she does not appear to be drunk as an evening of heavy drinking goes on, she "first lost her power of speech and just sat and listened, then she lost her sight and saw nothing that went on, and finally she ceased to hear" (202a, galley 2).

In spite of their weaknesses, Brett and Mike do pass the time fairly pleasantly in Paris, at least until Mike is called home to Scotland and Brett is left alone. Jake, anticipating her involvement with Robert Cohn, ends the first chapter on this note: "She had never been very good at being alone" (202a, galley 2). The tone of the chapter is very much introductory; as yet we are completely within the mind of Jake Barnes or Ernest Hemingway, still far from the action of the novel. (The suggestion that the voice of Jake has not been established here runs against the bitter irony of the early part of the chapter, but the suggestion is in accordance with such clues as the treatment of "Jake Barnes" in the third person, and the omission of any personal pronouns.)

Fitzgerald did not zero in on this particular characteristic of the first chapter, though its effect is perhaps included within his comment upon the preferability of the imagined to the seen or recounted. But he is strong in his denunciation of less-than-wholly-realized elements, calling some specific phrases "O. Henry stuff" and "mere horseshit" and finding the narration full of "about 24 sneers, superiorities and nose-thumbings-at-nothing" up to the beginning of the published chapter 3. His page references do not correspond to the galleys (only three galleys were deleted, and all of the material that Fitzgerald suggested should be eliminated would not have filled more than five or six galleys). Nor do they match the notebooks of the first draft, within which Young and Mann first discovered Fitzgerald's letter to Hemingway, because the pages of the notebook were not numbered. However, his references (with regard to quotes and page numbers) to pages 1, 2, 3, 5, 8, 9, 10, 14, 23, 30, 64, 65, 77, 78, and 87 (in some of the later references, Fitzgerald is praising, rather than complaining) match exactly the pagination of the typists' transcript of the first half of the final draft (item 200) and carbon copies of it (item 201 in the collection at the Kennedy Library; items 10208 and 10209 at the University of Virginia). Possibly supporting the other evidence that Fitzgerald actually read the Kennedy carbon copy (201) rather than the typists' original (200) or the Virginia typescript is the fact that in his letter he refers to the phrases " '9 or 14' and 'or how many years it was since 19xx' "; both phrases appear in the carbon copy, but the first has been inked out by Hemingway in the original typescript, possibly reflecting his own revision before he received Fitzgerald's critique.

In the second chapter of the typescript and of the canceled galley version, Jake's voice becomes more clearly defined. The chapter begins with the polished version of his discussion of why he is writing in the first person, "I did not want to tell this story in the first person," which I quoted earlier in regard to the narrative scheme of the novel (see p. 34 above). From this discussion of his emotional involvement with the characters and events of his story, Jake goes on to tell of his own background and motives:

> So my name is Jacob Barnes and I am writing the story, not as I believe is usual in these cases, from a desire for confession, because being a Roman Catholic I am spared that Protestant urge to literary production, nor to set things all out the way they happened for the good of some future generation, nor any other of the usual highly moral urges, but because I believe it is a good story. [202a, galley 2]

Fitzgerald's comment was: "If this paragraph isn't maladroit then I'm a rewrite man for Dr. [Samuel] Cadman [a popular theologian]." Jake goes on to say that he is "a newspaper man living in Paris," and he explains why Paris is the only city he would want to live in, in a manner that parallels Hemingway's later evocation of an idyllic Paris in *A Moveable Feast*. Jake has been discharged from the British hospital where he met Brett in 1916, and after having taken a job on the *New York Mail*, he has gone into partnership to start the Continental Press Association, of which he now serves as European director: "When you have a title like that, translated into French on the letter-heads, and only have to work about four or five hours a day and all the salary you want you are pretty well fixed." Jake is careful to keep that salary low enough so that not too many other newspapermen will try for his job. And now, leading a fairly contented life, he has decided to write the novel that all newspapermen want to write: "I suppose, now that I am doing it, the novel will have that awful taking-the-pen-in-hand quality that afflicts newspaper men when they start to write on their own hook" (202a, galley 2).

Jake goes on to discuss the quarter as a place where he had not spent much time until Brett and Mike came to Paris. It is important mostly because Robert Cohn, "one of the non-Nordic heroes of this book, had spent two years there" (202a, galley 2). The quarter is important because of its influence on Robert Cohn. Jake mentions Robert's mistress and Robert's novel ("There was a great deal of fantasy in it"), and then Jake goes on to recount the story of Ford Madox Ford's misidentification of Aleister Crowley which finally appeared in 1964 as the ninth chapter of *A Moveable Feast*. But as Jake illuminates the character of Robert Cohn, Jake again protests that Braddocks (Ford) is important only as the quarter is important:

> So I have never felt quite the same about Braddocks since, and I should avoid as far as possible putting him into this story except that he was a great friend of Robert Cohn, and Cohn is the hero.
> Robert Cohn was middleweight boxing champion of Princeton. Do not think that I am very much impressed by that as a boxing title, but it meant a lot to Cohn. [202a, galley 3]

Fitzgerald considered the introduction of Robert Cohn "a false start" and suggested, "Why not cut the inessentials in Cohens biography?" Hemingway did cut out some. Fitzgerald indicated his opinion about where the novel should begin:

> From here. Or rather from p. 30 [beginning of the published chapter 3] I began to like the novel but Ernest I can't tell you the sense of disappointment that beginning with its elephantine facetiousness gave me. Please do what you can about it in proof. Its 7500 words—you could reduce it to 5000. And my advice is not to do it by mere pareing but to take out the worst of the *scenes*.

Hemingway cut more deeply than Fitzgerald had advised, removing about thirty-five hundred words, but still choosing to include a good deal of information on Robert Cohn, thus half confirming his narrator's judgment that "Cohn is the hero," or at least one of the book's multiple imperfect heroes. Fitzgerald apparently had envisioned a considerable abridgment of the first two chapters of the typescript rather than the complete excision of the beginning material, for even near the end of his letter he is commenting upon small details in a way that would not be germane if he himself had been proposing a complete cut; for example, he takes Hemingway to task for having dysentery be the cause of the death of Brett's first love, using this as a cliché to avoid the equal cliché of his having been killed in the war. Fitzgerald's influence upon Hemingway is probably stronger in regard to Brett, who is not introduced until chapter 3 in the published novel, when she shows up at the *bal musette*. Fitzgerald called her character "elusive" and felt that "she dramatized herself in terms of [Michael] Arlen's dramatization of someone's dramatization of Stephen McKenna's dramatization of Diana Manner's dramatization of the last girl in Well's [*sic*] *Tono Bungay*." That is, in her actions, Brett seems very much indebted to other fictional and actual ladies of café society.

After deciding to cut to the middle of the second chapter, beginning with Robert Cohn, Hemingway still felt the impulse to include Brett in the book's beginning. So he typed a brief trial beginning to explain the missing material. This brief typescript begins with the same paragraph with which the uncut version began, explaining that the novel is about Lady Ashley and is set in Paris in the spring. It then goes on to explain:

> There were about [illegible passage crossed out] twenty five more pages like that which have ~~now~~ been cut out of this novel which now opens with Robert Cohn who ~~will~~ may be a great disappointment to the reader who has just been promised Lady Ashley. But if the reader will stay around Lady Ashley will come into the story again in a little while and will stay in until the end. A large amount of material about the author has also been cut out in the twenty five pages that have been eliminated and I feel sure that this will compensate the reader for any loss he may feel about Lady Ashley. ~~The only thing~~ We will now start with Robert Cohn. [202d]

It is evident from the reference to "twenty five more pages" that Hemingway was writing with a carbon copy of the typescript before him; that number of pages would take the reader to the introduction of Cohn in the typescript. It also seems likely that Hemingway was overestimating the appeal of Brett's title as a device for catching the reader's attention. In the published first chapter, a very short chapter, Jake's exposition of Cohn's background—family, literary, and marital—shades quickly into a discussion of his relationship with Frances Clyne and the dramatization of Frances's jealousy of Cohn, when Robert kicks Jake under the table. Chapter 2 follows a similar pattern, moving from Jake's discussion of Robert's romanticism to its dramatization in the two men's conversation about traveling to South America and Robert's comment, "Don't you ever get the feeling that all your life is going by" (*SAR*, p. 11). In these two chapters, Hemingway preserves something of the casual tone of the beginning of the typescript while he avoids

This is a novel about a lady . ~~She does not appear~~
~~until about twenty pages . Originally the book started off with it~~
Her name is Lady Ashley and when the story begins she is living
in Paris and it is Spring . That should be a good setting for a
romantic but highly moral story . As every one knows Paris is a
very romantic place . Spring in Paris is a very happy and
romantic time . Autumn in Paris , although very beautiful , might
give a note of sadness or melancholy that we shall try to keep
out of this story .
                              twenty
          There were about ~~twenty~~ five   more pages like that
which have ~~now~~ been cut out of this novel which now opens with
                    may
Robert Cohn who ~~will~~ be a great disappointment to the reader who
                              if the reader will stay around
has just been promised Lady Ashley . But/Lady Ashley will
come into the story again in a little while and will stay in
until the end . A large amount of material about the author
has also been cut out in the twenty five pages that have been
eliminated and I feel sure that this will compensate the reader
for any loss he may feel about Lady Ashley . ~~The only thing~~ We
will now start with Robert Cohn .

This is a trial beginning in which Hemingway considered the excision of the galley-proof beginning to the novel. This summary, which echoes the tone of the cut material, was never published (202d).

elements that Fitzgerald justifiably identified as being marked by "condescending *casuallness.*" And he moves quickly from an exposition that piques the reader's curiosity about Cohn to his much stronger dramatization of tensions within Cohn's character; at the same time he maintains a voice that is consistently identifiable as that of Jake Barnes.

Given the strengths of these two chapters in comparison to the weaknesses of the earlier chapters that were cut, the trial beginning of the typescript is clearly unnecessary: by referring to the cut chapters it merely capsulizes the faults of those chapters. Though Fitzgerald called the sections on Robert Cohn a "false start," preferring the entirely dramatized chapter 3 as the section in which "it really gets going,'' Hemingway was not content to abandon entirely the introductory tone that marked the material that he cut from the galley proofs.

That introductory tone was also obvious in another of Hemingway's trials, an introduction that derived its central image from the second quotation he chose as one of the book's two epigraphs. Just above the long passage from Ecclesiastes, this quotation was added in ink to the typescript version: ''You are all a lost generation.'' It is identified as having been spoken by Gertrude Stein, but its complete origins are revealed in the Foreword to what he then called ''The Lost Generation: *A Novel*'' (202c).

As he worked to choose the novel's final title, both in the Stein anecdote, used first as a foreword, and later as source for the novel's first epigraph and in a listing of possible titles, Hemingway chose to emphasize the optimistic idea of progress within life's cycle. It seems highly probable, though not perhaps completely proveable, that the notebook containing both the foreword and the list of titles, though it represents late material, came chronologically earlier than Fitzgerald's letter and the subsequent cuts in the novel's beginning, probably before the typescript was sent to Scribner's. This seems particularly likely, since the novel's typescript is titled *The Sun Also Rises* and since the quotation from Stein, ''You are all a lost generation,'' was written into the typescript by hand above the typed epigraph quotation from Ecclesiastes.

Handwritten within yet another of Hemingway's ubiquitous notebooks (this one dated 27 September 1925), the foreword tells the reader that ''One day last summer Gertrude Stein stopped in a garage in a small town in the Department of Ain to have a valve fixed in her Ford car'' (202c-1). After the repairs have been efficiently completed by one of several young mechanics at the garage, Miss Stein remarks to the proprietor that she thought ''you couldn't get boys to work any more.'' The owner informs her that good young workers can indeed be found—''It is the ones between twenty two and thirty that are no good. C'est un generation perdu [that is a lost generation]'' (202c-1). Only those who had fought in the war were lost.

From that anecdote, which Hemingway tells in about 150 words, he moves to a discussion of the titling of his novel. He had not heard the Gertrude Stein story until after he had finished his book, which he first wanted to call *Fiesta* (British editions of the book have appeared under that name from its publication to the present). He did not want to use a foreign title like *Fiesta,* and *Perdu* would lose ''a little something by being translated into lost'' (202c-2). From the discussion of titling, Hemingway used the word *lost* as a bridge into a discussion of his generation, which he sees as unique, unlike any generation whose future has been subject to past ''literary speculation.''

> This is not a question of what kind of mothers will flappers make or where is bobbed hair leading us. This is about something that is already finished. For whatever is going to happen to the generation of which I am a part has already happened. [202c-2]

Title.
The Sun also Rises.
~~Notes for the~~ Foreword.

For in much wisdom is much grief and
he that increase knowledge increaseth sorrow.
Two for the...
The old ; leaven.

The Lost Generation
A Novel.

Foreword.

One day last summer
Gertrude Stein stopped in a garage in
a small town in the Department of
Ain to have a valve ground in her
Ford car. The young mechanic who ~~worked~~
fixed it was very good. There were
three ~~other~~ other mechanics all about the
same age in the garage.

"Where do you get boys to work
like that?" Miss Stein asked the owner of
the garage. "I thought you couldn't get boys
to work any more."

"Oh yes," the garage owner
said. "You can get very good boys now.
I've taken all these and trained them myself.
It is the ones between twenty two
and thirty that are no good. C'est un
generation perdu. No one wants them.
They are no good. They were
spoiled. The young ones, the new ones
are all right again. ~~But you are trustant~~

In a projected foreword to his novel, Hemingway considered telling how Gertrude Stein came upon the term "The Lost Generation." On the facing page, he considered possible titles and an epigraph (202c-1).

In spite of all that will happen to the generation, in spite of all the movements it will seek salvation in, and in spite of the possibility of "another and better" war, nothing will really matter to this generation; it has been permanently shaped by its experience in the World War, an event already past. To this generation, Hemingway concludes, "the things that are given to people to happen to them have already happened" (202c-3).

At once, that judgment seems both to confirm and to falsify the structure of meaning that typifies *The Sun Also Rises*. Certainly, many of the characters have been marked by their experiences in the Great War, as permanently imprinted by its psychological effects as by the physical wounds it has inflicted on some of them. From it they have derived an essential toughness and skepticism which is seen most clearly in opposition to the unrealistic romanticism of Robert Cohn, who did not experience the war firsthand. In considering the titling in this foreword, Hemingway explored titles that would reflect the sense of a generation forever scarred by its experience: *The Lost Generation, Perdu, Lost.*

Elsewhere in the same notebook, he listed other titles, which were based on a reading of the Bible. At the head of the list was the title eventually selected, *The Sun Also Rises,* which derives from the first chapter of Ecclesiastes, where the Preacher considers man's "Vanity of vanities." The typescript of the novel also included the second verse from Ecclesiastes 1: "Vanity of vanities, saith the Preacher, vanity of vanities; all is vanity. . . ." (201; Hemingway's ellipsis), quoted as part of the epigraph. Beginning with the third printing of the novel, Hemingway eliminated that portion of the biblical quotation, which tends to confirm that he very consciously decided to set the second quote as a more optimistic alternative to Stein's statement. "That makes it much clearer. The point of the book to me was that the earth abideth forever," Hemingway wrote on 19 November 1926 in a letter to Maxwell Perkins requesting him to make the change.

The next title on this list is *River to the Sea,* which derives from Ecclesiastes 1:7, eventually quoted as part of the novel's second epigraph: "All the rivers run into the sea; yet the sea is not full; unto the place from whence the rivers come, thither they return again." Although in the context of Ecclesiastes both titles partially serve to characterize the vanity of man's sense of self-importance, as a part of the second epigraph each seems to suggest that the "lost generation" is not really lost, that it is only a part of the cycle of life and that if the sun has set upon the members of Jake's generation, it has set only for a while and, in the cycle of nature, will rise again. Hemingway later commented that those who viewed *The Sun Also Rises* as a pessimistic work ignored a great deal of the novel's content; Hemingway specifically commented upon the optimism of the second epigraph.

In this list of titles, Hemingway apparently also considered another possible epigraph—a less optimistic one. He wrote in a quotation from Ecclesiastes 1:18: "For in much wisdom is much grief and he that ~~increases~~ increaseth knowledge increaseth sorrow" (202c, inside back cover). This possible epigraph, of course, at once suggests one reason for the unhappiness of many of the book's characters—

The original dust jacket for *The Sun Also Rises* (1926)

their knowledge of the world has increased dramatically and traumatically during their experience of the war—and also ties in with the theme of compensation in *The Sun Also Rises,* which is clearly expressed in Jake's late-night conclusion that "you paid some way for everything that was any good" (*SAR,* p. 148).

The last of the titles drawn from Ecclesiastes derives from chapter four of that book, which contains a long discussion of the strength of two in comparison to the weaknesses of one. The chapter does not deal as a whole with "two" as an expression of sexual pairing, rather it discusses all the ways in which being allied with another person is a source of strength; but in the exact source of the title *Two Lie Together,* the reference may be more explicit: "Again, if two lie together, then they have heat: but how can one be warm alone?" (Ecclesiastes 4:11). Such heat, in its connotations of both sexual expression and comfortable closeness, is precisely what is denied to Jake and what is often treated without due respect by other characters. (By the end of the novel it may be that, insofar as is possible, Jake and Brett do "lie together" in the closeness of their mutual understanding.)

The last of the trial titles listed on the notebook page is probably the most obscure in its reference, *The Old Leaven.* While leaven is variously considered in the Bible, the "old leaven" is treated in the First Letter to the Corinthians, in a blending of the imagery of Christian rebirth with the Judaic preparations for the festival of Passover:

> Purge out therefore the old leaven, that ye may be a new lump, as ye are unleavened. For even Christ our passover is sacrificed for us: Therefore let us keep the feast, not with old leaven, neither with the leaven of malice and wickedness; but with the unleavened bread of sincerity and truth. [1 Corinthians 5:7,8]

Such a title would have placed its emphasis onto the negative side of the cycle of life. And while many of those who celebrate the festival of San Fermin are tainted by malice and wickedness, there are many positive characters, and even the most malicious of the book's main characters is not made wholly evil. Leaven has the property of making the part become the whole; one lump of it leavens the whole loaf. But in Hemingway's novel, evil is balanced by good; wisdom is gained, though at the price of vexation; the sea is never filled; life continues; and the sun goes down, but it also rises.

7

The Significance of *The Sun Also Rises*

More so than with any of his preceding works, the submerged base of Hemingway's narrative iceberg became important in the shaping of *The Sun Also Rises*. His statement that at least seven-eighths of a work may be left below the surface yet still exert its influence on the finished work, though it may not quite be literally true by weight of manuscript or count of pages, is a highly appropriate metaphor for describing the novel's composition. As Hemingway later wrote, "I had to take the first draft of *The Sun Also Rises* which I had written in one sprint of six weeks, and make it into a novel" (*MF,* p. 202). In the revision of his first novel he may not have been so drastically selective as in the composition of a much later masterwork, *The Old Man and the Sea*, which he said could have been a novel of many hundreds of pages, covering far more material than the old man, the boy, the great fish, and the sea. But by all the evidence, *The Sun Also Rises* is a highly selective work. He took a first draft and made it into a novel. It is the first work in which Hemingway's process of selection was both highly developed and can be so closely traced. It is also the first work in which we see his inherent respect for selective craftsmanship applied to the form of the novel.

Hemingway's earlier emphasis on such craftsmanship is evident in a later description (in his memoir *A Moveable Feast*) of "trying with great difficulty to write paragraphs that would be the distillation of what made a novel" (p. 75). Hemingway had practiced selection and deletion in earlier stories such as "Indian Camp" and "Big Two-Hearted River" and in the composition of the chapters of *In Our Time*, the paragraphs that he mentions. *The Sun Also Rises* was the masterwork with which Hemingway proclaimed that his journeyman efforts were completely at an end; his method of composition had been perfected.

In this novel, Hemingway confronted the difficulty of achieving a crafts-manlike artistry within a long form. His final achievement resulted partly from his earlier work in very short stories and poetry, from his work toward longer forms in such pieces as "Big Two-Hearted River," and from all the fluency that he had developed in his early writing, from journalism to the manuscript of a novel that Hadley had lost on the train to Switzerland. In *The Sun Also Rises,* the methods that he had defined earlier were developed and polished. Although, like so much of Hemingway's other writing, the novel seems to be simple in language and structure, its underlying complexity is apparent to the careful reader and is even more apparent when one examines its manuscript drafts. Hemingway struggled for the appearance of simplicity in the novel, striving for a prose that will work on his readers with the subtlety normally associated with such a genre as poetry. He aims for such a subtle simplicity, not in order to create a tour de force, but in order to re-create the experiences of life and to show the effects that those experiences have on men and women. As he wrote in an unpublished draft for *A Moveable Feast* (179-1), he found himself trying

> to make something that will become a part of the readers experience and a part of his memory. There must be things that he did not notice when he read the story or the novel which, without his knowing it, enter into his memory and experience so that they are a part of his life. This is not easy to do.

Proof of the difficulty of his task appears in the drafts of *The Sun Also Rises,* in such revisions as the reduction of nine lines of dialogue to three in the love scene between Jake and Brett, the complete rewriting of Romero's *recibiéndo* killing of the bull, or the elimination of the description of the Ledoux–Kid Francis fight.

Hemingway's task of composing and revision was at once eased and complicated by the novel's appearing to be a *roman à clef.* While the characters in the novel sometimes resemble real people, Brett Ashley is not Duff Twysden; Robert Cohn is not Harold Loeb; and Jake Barnes is not Ernest Hemingway. The tendency in building on the events of June 1925 might have been merely to transcribe from the events of real life: certainly, that would have been an easy course to follow, but it was not the course that Hemingway had to follow in order to come to his maturity as a novelist. Instead, the events of that June provided him less with an outline and cast for his novel than with an initial impulse, upon which he expanded and rang changes. He did not simply describe one trip into Spain; he synthesized from all his experiences of Spain, telescoping scenes and events that he derived from several trips to Spain over a period of years. After only a few pages of his first draft he had already begun to transform and fictionalize his characters; he began to omit references to such real people as Dos Passos, Fitzgerald, and Ford and continued the process of fictionalizing the characters through the successive drafts of *The Sun Also Rises.* He worked to re-create his material in a manner that derived directly from his belief in the superiority of the imagined to the merely described. Even before he began the novel he had written, "The only writing that was any good was what you made up, what you imagined" (draft of "Big Two-Hearted River," published as "On Writing" in *NAS*, p. 237). Each revision he made helped to underline that principle; he moved toward a completely realized fictional whole.

The process of fictionalization began early in *The Sun Also Rises;* after the first thirty or so pages of the first draft, the book had clearly been established as a work of fiction. Yet Hemingway's efforts to "imagine" the book continued throughout, forming some of the most interesting—to anyone who is concerned with Hemingway's aesthetic and technique—of the passages that he later cut from the novel's drafts, the passages in which Hemingway directly comments upon his aims and the difficulties that he is having in achieving those aims. Hemingway's concern that no "conventional literary signs" mark the book's important sections, linked with the conviction that for maximum effect the elements of the work must enter the reader's experience imperceptibly, eventually led him to cut these discussions; nevertheless, they clearly demonstrate and underscore a number of his concerns. Hemingway reacted against the conventional formulaic fiction of his time, with its unrealistic romanticism, and he strove to escape the existing conventions of middle-class thought. He wished to reflect the complexities of life, yet to do so with great precision. Such aims are reflected in, for example, his effort to achieve a complexity in characterization—to present a number of partial "heroes" in *The Sun Also Rises*. They are reflected in his work to avoid abstraction whenever possible and in his accompanying pursuit of a concrete and honest use of language. Hemingway worked so precisely with language not merely because he desired a carefully crafted surface for his work but also because of his conviction that only in a carefully controlled art can truthful insight be achieved.

The discussions that he later cut from the drafts of the novel also treat at length with difficulties of narration. Hemingway particularly was commenting on the difficulty of achieving a suitably objective narration from a first-person point of view. Yet his experiments soon showed him that it was impossible to find an immediate and objective narration within a third-person framework. The story takes its own directions and imposes its own organic imperatives, and it "must" be told in the first person. As he developed the novel, Hemingway noved away from—or at least readapted—many of the techniques that he had used in his earlier short fiction. His adoption of a first-person narration, for example, was in contrast to the third-person presentation of most of his earlier stories, moving him away from a "splendid and cool and detached" stance. He balanced that movement carefully in his acute consciousness of the role of irony as a balance, thus ensuring that Jake Barnes's telling of *The Sun Also Rises* will not become so subjective as to imperil the truthfulness of the presentation.

Hemingway also chose not to use the *in medias res* opening with which he began the first draft. By changing the beginning, he not only adopted a more leisurely, chronological narration which was better suited to the amount of material that he had to handle in a novel; he also balanced his presentation, contrasting the workaday Jake Barnes of the earlier sections to the narrator Jake Barnes in the midst of the swirling fiesta. When they know more about Jake's involvements and sympathies, readers are better able to judge the varying objectivity of his narration.

Hemingway also built upon his early short fiction as he edited and developed his novel. Such scenes as the intense paragraphs of *in our time* had earlier been written as complete units in themselves. Later these scenes were reordered and juxtaposed with longer stories as the chapters of *In Our Time*. In *The Sun Also Rises*, similar scenes were conceived and written as part of the complete longer work, and sometimes they were ruthlessly edited out when they were not organic to the flow of plot, theme, characterization, and other elements of the novel. Thus, Hemingway carefully developed the novel's bullfight scenes while cutting the similarly exciting and immediate description of the Ledoux–Kid Francis prize fight to only a mention. In Romero's corridas, the plot, theme, and characterization are all served; the prize fight worked thematically in much the same way as the bullfights, but it contributed little else to the overall structure of the novel. Such selection is continually at work in Hemingway's writing of the novel; it shows—as it should—a far tighter organization than *In Our Time*.

If the chapters of *In Our Time* were Hemingway's distillation of what makes a novel, then the process of writing a complete novel was a continuing process of selection, blending, and fermentation—not the distillation of a liqueur, but the production of a fine wine which can only mellow and improve with age, its taste at once more subtle and yet more sustained. Hemingway's vision and revision of his novel, then, involved attention both to its largest and to its tiniest elements. He sometimes scrapped and replaced entire scenes and chapters. He deleted the beginning chapters, parts of which were used much later in *A Moveable Feast*. He rewrote Romero's corridas, dropped the description of the prize fight, and eliminated his retelling of A. E. W. Mason's story. And, of course, he cut the discussions about his intention and technique. These changes and a number of others were made with the aim of "trying to hold this pretty tight down to the story" (198), trying to produce a tightly unified work. Hemingway also paid close attention to the language of the novel, carefully tuning words and phrases with a concern that was more poetic than novelistic. Consider, for example, the haunting, insistent repetition of individual words in the discussion of Vicente Girones's death. Consider the paring away of maudlin dialogue until Jake and Brett's discussion of their frustrated love suggests, in its terse restraint, the inescapable barriers between the two. This careful fitting of word to meaning is continually evident in the revision of the novel, and it helps to suggest why Hemingway thought that the task was, "the most difficult job of rewriting I have ever done" (*MF*, p. 202).

In *The Sun Also Rises*, Hemingway demonstrated his mastery over all the skills he had practiced and perfected in his earlier work. The book, perhaps more importantly, shows his maturation into an artist of the first rank in his ability to integrate and interrelate all the varied elements of the novel, subordinating each to the overall effects he aimed to achieve, emphasizing or playing down each as his material required, but never losing sight of the whole. Before *The Sun Also Rises*, Ernest Hemingway had promised much—perhaps even greatness. With this novel he achieved that greatness and gave promise of continuing achievements to come.

Appendixes

A: THE MANUSCRIPTS DESCRIBED

MANUSCRIPT AND TYPESCRIPT VERSIONS OF *THE SUN ALSO RISES* IN THE JOHN F. KENNEDY LIBRARY (KEYED TO HEMINGWAY COLLECTION IDENTIFICATION NUMBERS)

The First Draft

193 and 194—THE FIRST DRAFT—handwritten by Hemingway between 21 July and 21 September 1925

(193)—THE LOOSE-SHEET BEGINNING—thirty-two sheets of letter-sized paper, which continues in the notebooks. Also included with item 193 are two additional typescript sheets that Hemingway later added to precede the draft. The first of these pages introduces an early (misquoted) epigraph: "Facing Page one of Chapter One The grave's a fine and secret [*sic*] place / But none I think do there embrace. . . . . / Marvell." The second page represents Hemingway's working out of the characters' names—not the names used in the first draft, but the ones that appeared in the finished novel.

(194)—THE NOTEBOOKS—the balance of the first draft. There are seven of these small notebooks, index numbered JFK 194-1 through JFK 194-6. The seventh notebook includes only a few pages of text and is actually filed with

```
                              Original name
                                       Neil
                            Lady Elizabeth Brett  Murray

       Names   for Duff ----     LadyxxBork

                                               Ashley
                               Married       Burkxx
                                      Robert  Lambertxx
                                Lord Henry Mariane
                                               Ashley
                          Name  generally used  Brett  Lambertxx


   Other characters    Bill  Gorton

                       Gerald Cohn

                       Mike   Campbell

                       Jake  Barnes

                       Harvey Stone
```

Hemingway's choice of names for the characters (193)

notebook 6 and indexed as items 194-6-52 through 194-6-57. On the front cover of each of these small notebooks (of the type used by schoolchildren), Hemingway wrote the name of the city in which he was working and (on the first four) the dates on which he wrote in it. Each of the final three notebooks includes only a single date.

The Typescript "Second" Draft

198, 199, 200, 201—THE TYPESCRIPT DRAFT—incorporates most of the changes Hemingway made while revising his manuscript at Schruns, Austria, during "the winter of the avalanches," 1925/26. This typescript draft actually is a composite draft, composed partially of a Hemingway typescript and partially of a typist's transcription of a portion of the novel that is not covered by Hemingway's transcript. Also included and indexed in the collection at the Kennedy Library are two carbon copies of typists' versions. Neither of these carbon copies includes any handwritten corrections, but such corrections are included both on Hemingway's and on the typists' originals.

TABLE A.A.1
THE FIRST DRAFT

JFK Index	Item	Location/ Date	Number of Pages	Corresponding Pages in SAR
193	Beginning on loose sheets (undated)[a]		32[b]	163–64, 171–78[c]
194-1	Notebook 1	Valencia/July 23– August 3	92	1–36[d]
194-2	Notebook 2	Valencia/August 3 Madrid/August 5, 6 San Sebastián/ August 8, 9 Hendaya/August 10, 11, 12	80	36–72
194-3	Notebook 3[e]	Hendaya/August 12, 13, 14, 15, 16, 17 Paris/August 19, 20	80	74–116
194-4	Notebook 4[f]	Paris/August 20, 21, 22, 23, 24, 25, 26, 27, 28, 29	100	116–54
194-5	Notebook 5	Paris/"Finished Sept 9"	92	154–62, 164–71, 178–206
194-6	Notebook 6[g]	Paris/September 9	74	207–45
	Notebook 7[h]	Paris/September 21, 1925	5	245–47

[a] Hemingway later said that he had begun the novel on his birthday, July 21: see the 1 April 1951 letter to Carlos Baker and the interview in the *Paris Review* in 1958. While Baker discounts the July 21 starting date, given the July 23 dating of notebook 1, the birthday beginning date is perfectly reasonable in light of the number of pages that Hemingway completed before he began to work in the notebooks. Only the fact that the letter to Baker is dated April Fool's Day might lead us to suspect Hemingway's veracity.
[b] Two other sheets, described above, are also indexed as a part of 193, but these probably were added later in the process of composition.
[c] The loose sheets, which were greatly altered in the process of revision, include a very long version of the meeting with the American ambassador.
[d] A good deal of material derived from notebook 1 was deleted in the galley proofs of *The Sun Also Rises,* at least partially at the suggestion of F. Scott Fitzgerald. [Cont. p. 118.]

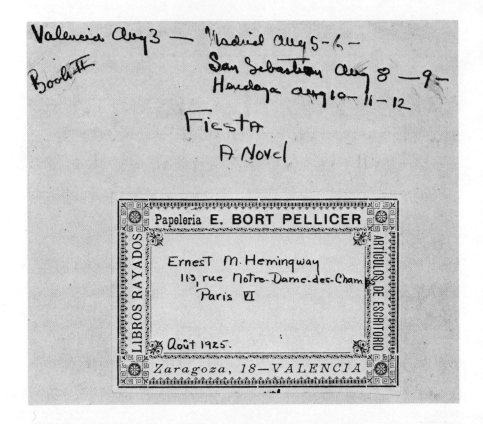

(200)—The first section of the typescript draft is represented by a 122-page TYPISTS' VERSION of the first eight (as published) chapters of *The Sun Also Rises*. This typescript begins with the first chapter and a half, which was later cut from the galley proofs, and is divided into ten chapters. It includes a few minor corrections in Hemingway's hand, as well as a considerable reworking of the Jake/Brett love scene that appears on page 55 of the final novel. The Gertrude Stein epigraph has been inserted by hand on the title page.

---

[e] On its back cover, notebook 3 includes a word count, notations of travel expenses, and an outline of the projected structure of the rest of the novel.

[f] On the back cover are notes, addresses for William Groule, and a very rough map of the Great Lakes.

[g] The last page contains a partial draft of a letter to the editor (of the *Toronto Star?*), apparently in Hadley Hemingway's handwriting. The letter deals with receiving a bull's ear. (The section in which Duff/Brett receives the bull's ear from Romero is included in notebook 5.)

[h] The last three pages of the notebook contain the draft of a passage in which Jake examines his relationship with Brett. Later cut, a smoother version of this passage appears as the beginning of Book II of the typescript version of the novel.

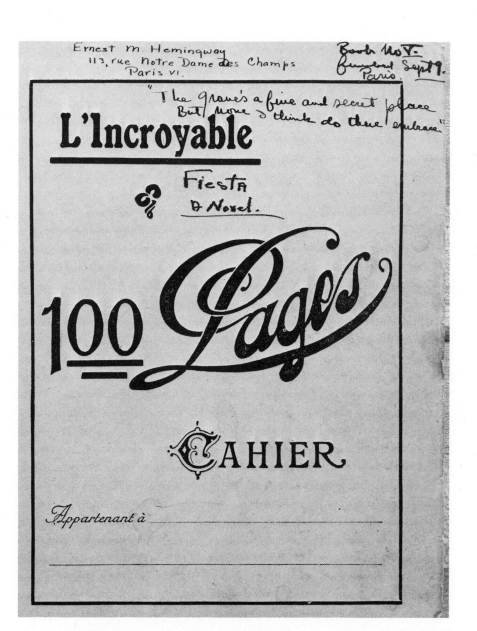

Covers (above and on facing page) from two of the seven notebooks in which
Hemingway wrote most of the first draft of his novel, then titled *Fiesta* (194-2-1
and 194-5-1)

" Well ," I said." It can't hurt Marcial any ."

" Marcial has been in San Sebastian all day . Themndnomm
He drove over in a car this morning with Marquez . I don't think
they'll be back tonight ."

Montoya stood embarrassed . He wanted me to say something .

" Don't give Romero the message ," I said.

" You think so ?"

" Absolutely ."

Montoya was very pleased .

" I wanted to ask you because you were an American ," he
said.

" That's what I'd do ."

" Look," said Montoya ." People take a boy like that . They
don't know whatkm he's worth . They don't know what he means . Any
foreigner can flatter him . They start this Grand Hotel business and in
one year they're through ."

" Like Algabeno ," I said.

" Yes. Like Algabeno ."

" They're a fine lot ," I said. "There's one American
woman down here now that collects bull fighters . "

" I know . They only want the young ones."

" Yes," I said." The old ones get fat ."

" Or crazy like Gallo ."

" Well," I said. "It's easy . All you have to do is not
give him the message ."

" He's such a fine boy ," said Montoya ." He ought to stay
with his own people .He shouldn't mix in that stuff."

" Won't you have a drink ?" I asked .

" No, saidx Montoya ." I have to go ."

A typical page of Hemingway's typescript of the second half of the novel,
showing his characteristic spacing around marks of punctuation and a short
addition to the text—typical of the changes made in this draft (198-2-100)

TABLE A.A.2

CHAPTER/BOOK COLLATION OF MAJOR DRAFTS OF "THE SUN ALSO RISES"
(This traces the divisions indicated in each draft.)

First Draft (193 & 194)	Hemingway's Typescript[a] (198)	Typists' Version[a] (200 & 201)	Published Version
—		—	Book I
—		Chapter 1	—(Deleted in galley stage
Chapter 2	(Not an exact correspondence. The typists' version of chap. 2	Chapter 2	—through the middle of chap. 2 of 200)
—		—	Chapter 1
Chapter 4	appears several pages later in the text than does the first draft of	Chapter 3 (There is no chap. 4 in 200 or 201)	Chapter 2
Chapter 5	chap. 2. Hemingway's	Chapter 5	Chapter 3
Chapter 6	typescript begins with	Chapter 6	Chapter 4
Chapter 7	the published chap. 9. It is numbered 1 but does not continue the numbering of the 200 draft)	(There is no chap. 7; chap. 8 is used twice)	Chapter 5
Chapter 8		Chapter 8	Chapter 6
Chapter 9		Chapter 9	Chapter 7
Chapter 10		(within preceding chapters)	
—		Book II	Book II
Chapter 11		Chapter 10	Chapter 8
Chapter 12	Chapter 11	(The typists' version	Chapter 9
Chapter 13	Chapter 12	runs only through the	Chapter 10
Chapter 14	Chapter 13	end of published chap.	Chapter 11
Chapter 15	Chapter 14	8)	Chapter 12
Chapter 16	Chapter 15		Chapter 13
Chapter 17	Chapter 16		Chapter 14
Chapter 18	Chapter 17		Chapter 15
—	Chapter 18[a]		(within chap. 15)[b]
—	Chapter 19		Chapter 17
—	Book III		Book III
Chapter 21	Chapter 22		Chapter 19
Chapter 22	Chapter 23[b]		(within chap. 19)[c]

[a] Chapter divisions in the Virginia Typescript draft, from which the type was set, essentially follow these drafts.
[b] The deleted chapter division would have come at the top of p. 164 of *The Sun Also Rises*. In Hemingway's typescript, chap. 17 ends just after Bill and Jake meet Romero, then [cont. p. 123]

The Sun Also Rises

Chapter One .

        I saw him for the first time in his room at the
Hotel Montoya in Pamplona .   Bill and I were going up to
our room to get the wine skin to take to the bull fight
and we met Montoya on the stairs . "̦ Come on," said Montoya ."
Would you like to meet Pedro Romero ?"

        ~~Wexfallowed~~
        "Let's go see him ," Bill said.
        We followed Montoya down the hall .

        "He's in room number eight," ⧖ Montoya explained .
" He's getting dressed for the bull fight ."

        Walking after Montoya down the corridor ~~pastcthe~~
~~glassd~~ I knew what room number eight was like inside . It
was a gloomy room with little light coming in from the
window on the narrow street .There were two beds separated by
a monastic partition . I had been lodged there the year before .
⧖ Montoya knocked and opened the door .

              The boy stood very straight and unsmiling in his
white shirt and gold pants .
His black hair shone under the electric light . He was dressed ,
except for his coat which lay on one of the beds , and his sash
had just been wound .He nodded seeming far away and dignified
when we shook hands . Montoya made a little speech about
what great lovers of bull fighting we were and how we wanted
to wish him luck . Romero listened very seriously .Then
he turned to me . He was the best looking boy I have ever seen .

        "You go to see the bull fight ," he said in English .

        "You know English," I said ,feeling like an idiot

A fairly late first-person version (opposite page and above) of the meeting
between Jake and Romero (195)

```
2
as I said it .

        "No," he answered and smiled .

        A Spanish newspaper man from San Sebastian  came up
and asked us if we spoke French . "Would you like me to interpret
for you? Is there anything you would like to askPedro Romero?"

        We thanked him . What was there that you would like
to ask? The boy was nineteen years old ,alone except for his
sword handler  and this newspaper man and the bull fight was
to commence in twenty minutes . We wished him,"Mucha Suerte,"
shook hands and went out of. He was standing ,straight and
handsome  and altogether by himself ,alone in the room with the
two hangers on  as we shut the door .

        "He's a fine boy .Don't you think so? " Montoya
asked .

        "He's a good looking kid ,'"
        "We'll see how he is in the ring ," Montoya said.

        We found the big leather wine bag leaning against
the wall in the room ,took it and the field glasses ,locked
the door  and went downstairs      ?
```

(201)—A CARBON COPY of (200)—without corrections or Stein epigraph.

(198)—The typescript draft is completed by the HEMINGWAY TYPESCRIPT of the second half of the novel, beginning with the published chapter 9. This typescript is marked by the author's characteristic style of typing— Hemingway usually leaves a space both before and after such marks of punctuation as commas and periods. Hemingway's typescript includes a number of corrections in his hand. Though this typescript represents a later

collect field glasses and wine bottles from their rooms, and go downstairs in the Hotel Montoya. Chap. 18 begins at the bullring, with the line "It was a good bull-fight."

c This second deleted chapter division comes just a few pages from the end of the book, at the bottom of p. 243 of *The Sun Also Rises*. Just before the chapter division, Brett restates her desire never to talk about having left Romero. The new chapter begins as Jake and Brett leave the Hotel Montana and discover that Brett's bill has been paid.

section of the novel than that contained in the typists' version, it carries a lower Kennedy Library index number under curator Jo August Hills's indexing system, which gives priority to Hemingway's own work.

Trial Beginnings

195, 197, 197a, 202c, & 202d—These TRIAL BEGINNINGS, some of which the Kennedy Library indexes as "false starts," are perhaps misrepresented by either term. A careful examination of the names that Hemingway assigned to characters in these short trials in comparison to the names that he used in other drafts reveals that none come earlier than JFK item 193, the "loose sheets" beginning to the first draft. In a note to chapter 4 of his biography of Hemingway, Carlos Baker identifies one of the typescript trial beginnings (either 197 or 197a, both of which begin "It was half past three in the afternoon" and continue in the third person) as having preceded the loose-sheet draft. However, both of these typescripts identify characters by names that were not established until late in the first draft of the novel. Continuing his note, Baker admits that "my view that these trial drafts precede the main draft is conjectural" (p. 589).

What these trial beginnings do represent is Hemingway's working out—at different stages in the composition of the novel, but probably no earlier than the completion of the first draft—of several apparent difficulties. These are alternative versions of already established beginnings; they are related to each other much as are the numerous trial endings of *A Farewell to Arms,* in which Hemingway explored two possible endings in some thirty-five different variations (Reynolds, p. 49).

While far fewer variations exist in the case of *The Sun Also Rises,* Hemingway explores three essentially different points of departure: in the first, the novel opens in Romero's room at the Hotel Montoya; in the second, it begins with a long expository section on the novel's characters (as in the typescript draft); in the third, Hemingway has cut a good deal of that second-draft exposition, beginning midway with an examination of Robert Cohn, after having cut his discussion of Jake, Brett, and others. This third beginning, of course, is the one that eventually appeared in the published novel.

(195, 197, 197a)—These three fragments, all in typescript, are reworkings of the novel's first beginning in the loose sheets of the first draft; they were probably composed between the notebook and typescript drafts of the novel, or even later, judging by the names assigned to characters. In these fragments, Hemingway did not use the names seen in the first draft. Draft 195 (2 pp.) seems to be a relatively late version; it is headed *"The Sun Also*

The Sun Also Rises

A Novel .

It was half past three in the afternoon in a dark
bedroom in the Hotel Montoya in Pamplona,Spain . It was a
cheap room because the boy who lived in it had not yet learned to
appreciate luxury . So far , that year , he had made sixty thousand
dollars . The money represented the measure of his success . He had
not yet had time to experiment with the things that money could
buy . He had an idea that at the end of the season , if he did not
go to Mexico , he would buy himself a motor car . He was nineteen
years old and he stood very straight , and very handsome and
quite alone although there were five people in his bedroom .

Pedro Romero was the boy's name and he was a bull fighter
. Two Americans on their way to their room to get a leather wine
bottle to take to the bull fight had met Montoya ,the proprietor of
the hotel ,on the stairs .

"Come on , Montoya said ."You ought to meet Pedro
Romero . He's just dressed for the bull fight ."

The two Americans were named William Gorton and Jacob
Barnes and they followed the proprietor of the hotel into the
dark bedroom where the boy stood ,dressed in his bull fighting
clothes , except for his coat which lay on one of the beds . He
stood ,very straight and unsmiling and the electric light shone on
his hair brushed very smooth and shiny from his brown face .
He nodded seeming very far away and dignified when he shook hands
with Barnes and Gorton . Montoya made a little speech about what
great admireress of bull fighting the two Americans were and how
they wanted to wish him luck . Romero listened very seriously .
Then he turned to Jake Barnes .

Hemingway's first attempt to handle *The Sun Also Rises* from a third-person
point of view (197)

The Sun Also Rises

A Novel .

It was half past three in the afternoon in a dark bedroom
in the Hotel Montoya in Pamplona , Spain . It was a cheap room ~~xxxxxx~~
because the boy who lived in it had not/learned to appreciate
yet
luxury. He stood under the electric light in the center of the
room and seemed quite alone altho there were five people in the
he
~~xxxxxx~~ bedroom . Two Spanish newspaper men sat on the bed .
They were amused . The boy , who was a bull fighter , was talking
English .

" You go to see the bull fight?" he asked the two
Americans who had just been introduced to him .

" You know English , " one of the Americans said ,feeling
as he said it what an idiotic remark it was.

" No . I only talk it a little ," he smiled . The
electric light shone on his hair . He was twenty years old and
very straight and handsome . Each afternoon that he killed bulls
and unsmiling .
he made seven thousand five hundred pesetas which is ~~xxxxxx~~ a
little over a thousand dollars . This year/he would make seventy
if nothing happened
thousand dollars . ~~Ifxnothingxhappenedxxx~~ Montoya , the owner
of the hotel made a little speech telling the boy what great lovers
of bull fighting the two Americans were . Pédro Romero listened
very seriously

Hemingway's second attempt at a third-person narration. Both attempts were
quickly abandoned (197a).

Rises/Chapter One.'' It is a first-person account from Jake's point of view, and it incorporates the character names used in the published novel.

Both draft 197 (1 p.) and draft 197a (5 pp.) represent Hemingway's attempt to recast his first-person narration into a third-person account. They lend substance to a statement made early in the second draft of the novel: ''I did not want to tell this story in the first person but I find that I must'' (200). Both 197 and 197a use the late character names; 197 is the earlier of the two, because words typed in above the lines of 197 are included within the lines of 197a. In 197, only events in Romero's bedroom are covered, while in 197a—the later (and smoother) version—the scene in the hotel is succeeded by a polished version of the first draft's meeting between the revelers and the American ambassador and his party.

The longer third-person trial (197a) is written from an omniscient viewpoint, including not only Jake's analysis of his anger at being persuaded by Brett to meet with the ambassador but also Romero's thoughts as he plans for his future—at the end of the season he will either go to Mexico or buy a motorcar. While the second of the third-person trials is not bad—certainly it is much more polished than its predecessor—it still represents a dead end in the composition of the novel. While it allows the reader to know what is in each character's mind, the third-person viewpoint seems flat and without tension by comparison to the first-person narration that Hemingway elected to retain.

(202c, 202d)—These two trial beginnings are related to both the second and third points of departure that Hemingway tried. More specifically, they represent Hemingway's attempt to replace or explain the deletion of the initial chapter and a half of the novel's chronological beginning, which was cut in the galley proofs of the novel. In 202d, a one-page typescript, Hemingway's narrator notes in beginning, ''This is a novel about a lady,'' starting it with the same sentence with which he began the second draft. But he then goes on to explain that about twenty-five pages have been cut and that the novel ''now opens with Robert Cohn who may be a great disappointment to the reader who has just been promised Lady Ashley.''

In 202c, within yet another of his notebooks, Hemingway began to write a Foreword to his novel, which he here called *The Lost Generation*. He recounted the story of a garage owner who, in a conversation with Gertrude Stein, identifies the young men who went through the World War as *un generation perdu*. Hemingway went on to maintain that ''to this generation . . . the things that are given to people to happen to them have already happened.'' It is unclear whether this unused introduction, datelined Chartres, 27 September 1925, was the source for or merely followed the ''lost generation'' quotation written in on the title page of item 200, the first half of the typescript draft. This notebook also includes a list of trial titles.

New chapter

Chapter VIII.

I did not see Brett again until she came back from San Sebastian. One card came from her from there. It had a picture of the Concha and said: "Darling. very quiet and healthy. love to all the chaps. Brett."

Nor did I see Robert Cohn again. Frances had left for England and I had a note from Cohn saying he was going out in the country for a couple of weeks, he did not know where, but that he wanted to hold me to the fishing trip in Spain we had talked about last winter. I could reach him always, he wrote, through his bankers. Brett Brett was gone, I was not bothered by Cohn's troubles, I rather enjoyed not having to play tennis, there was plenty of work to do, I went often to the races, lived with friends, and put in some extra time at the office getting things ahead so I could leave it in charge of my secretary when Bill Gorton and I shoved off to Spain the end of June. Bill Gorton arrived, put up a couple of days at the flat and went off to Vienna. He was very cheerful and said the states were wonderful.

An intermediate draft in which Hemingway worked on the beginning of chapter 8, adding material (at the beginning of the third paragraph) that summarizes Jake's activities (196)

You must make fantastic statements
to know things.

It is like living
with fourteen men so hd we will
know there is some one you love.

We cant do it you cant
hurt people. It's what we believe
in place of god.

I have to have it and I
cant have what I want much
you so I'm going to take this
other thing.

I have never been able to
have any thing I ever wanted.

And I knew it you and
I thought I wouldn't be able to stand
it.

What a clever he put the top thing
down just as he came up.

Well are you so merry about.
What were you so merry about the other
day.

On these two notebook pages (to the left and above),
Hemingway collected characteristic statements to be
worked into Brett's dialogue (202b).

Fragmentary Materials

195a, 196, 202, 202a, & 202b—These assorted fragments, none more than a few
pages long, represent various leftovers from the composition of *The Sun
Also Rises,* trial fragments in which Hemingway worked out various
problems. It is likely that other such fragments might exist and may yet be
found.

(195a)—a pre-notebook draft of the scene in which Jake and a waiter discuss the
death of Vicente Girones, the man who is gored during the running of the
bulls. This is an earlier draft than the one that appears in the notebooks,
judging from a comparison of words written in above the lines of 195a with
the same words within the lines of the notebook.

(196)—A draft of the beginning of chapter 8 of *The Sun Also Rises.* This
fragment of manuscript, which is very close to the final version published
on page 69 of the novel, included three and a half lines at the beginning of
the third paragraph that do not appear in the first draft.

(202 & 202a)—The original (202a) and a photocopy, including a few notes by
Philip Young (202), of the three long galley proofs that Hemingway cut
from the beginning of the novel.

(202b)—Yet another of Hemingway's notebooks, this one blank save for two
pages on which Hemingway has written seven or eight statements by Duff/
Brett. Several were worked into her dialogue in the finished novel.

THE TYPESCRIPT VERSION OF *THE SUN ALSO RISES* IN THE MANUSCRIPT DEPARTMENT OF THE UNIVERSITY OF VIRGINIA LIBRARY (KEYED TO THAT DEPARTMENT'S ACCESSION NUMBERS)

The Setting Copy

10208 & 10209—THE SETTING COPY of the novel, in two major sections,
which divide the novel in the same way that JFK items 200 and 198 divide
it. Both 10208 & 10209 are typists' transcriptions of the novel, while JFK
item 198 is Hemingway's own typescript of the latter section of the novel. It
is somewhat confusing to compare the JFK and the University of Virginia
typescripts; the confusion lessens if one bears in mind that the JFK item
numbers and the University of Virginia accession numbers do not identify
equivalent blocks of material.

(10208)—This accession number is used to identify fifteen pages of material very
recently added to the University of Virginia's collection. The pages
represent the material that was cut from the novel's beginning at the galley
stage.

(10209)—This accession number lumps two distinct typescripts, which together make up the text of *The Sun Also Rises* as published. The first typescript is a carbon copy of JFK item number 200; it begins with page 16, taking up where item 10208 left off. The second typescript is an original, a typist's version of Hemingway's typescript (JFK 198) which completes the text of the novel.

B: THE BEGINNING CUT FROM THE GALLEYS

Gal I—Hemingway's The Sun—51902————11-12-31

THE SUN ALSO RISES

———

BOOK I

CHAPTER I

THIS is a novel about a lady. Her name is Lady Ashley and when the story begins she is living in Paris and it is Spring. That should be a good setting for a romantic but highly moral story. As every one knows, Paris is a very romantic place. Spring in Paris is a very happy and romantic time. Autumn in Paris, although very beautiful, might give a note of sadness or melancholy that we shall try to keep out of this story.

Lady Ashley was born Elizabeth Brett Murray. Her title came from her second husband. She had divorced one husband for something or other, mutual consent; not until after he had put one of those notices in the papers stating that after this date he would not be responsible for any debt, etc. He was a Scotchman and found Brett much too expensive, especially as she had only married him to get rid of him and to get away from home. At present she had a legal separation from her second husband, who had the title, because he was a dipsomaniac, he having learned it in the North Sea commanding a mine-sweeper, Brett said. When he had gotten to be a proper thoroughgoing dipsomaniac and found that Brett did not love him he tried to kill her, and between times slept on the floor and was never sober and had great spells of crying. Brett always declared that it had been one of the really great mistakes of her life to have married a sailor. She should have known better, she said, but she had sent the one man she had wanted to marry off to Mesopotamia so he would last out the war, and he had died of some very unromantic form of dysentery and she certainly could not marry Jake Barnes, so when she had to marry she had married Lord Robert Ashley, who proceeded to become a dipsomaniac as before stated.

They had a son and Ashley would not divorce, and would not give grounds for divorce, but there was a separation and Brett went off with Mike Campbell to the

Continent one afternoon, she having offered to eat lunch because Mike was lonely and sick and very companionable, and, as she said, "obviously one of us." They arranged the whole business before the Folkestone-Boulogne train left London at 9:30 that night. Brett was always very proud of that. The speed with which they got passports and raised funds. They came to Paris on their way to the Riviera, and stayed the night in a hotel which had only one room free and that with a double bed. "We'd no idea of anything of that sort," Brett said. "Mike said we should go on and look up another hotel, but I said no, to stop where we were. What's the odds." That was how they happened to be living together.

Mike at that time was ill. It was all he had brought back with him from the two years he had spent in business in Spain, after he had left the army, except the beautifully engraved shares of the company which had absorbed all of the fifteen thousand pounds that had come to him from his father's estate. He was also an undischarged bankrupt, which is quite a serious thing in England, and had various habits that Brett felt sorry for, did not think a man should have, and cured by constant watchfulness and the exercise of her then very strong will.

Mike was a charming companion, one of the most charming. He was nice and he was weak and he had a certain very hard gentleness in him that could not be touched and that never disappeared until the liquor dissolved him entirely. Mike sober was nice, Mike a little drunk was even nicer, Mike quite drunk began to be objectionable, and Mike very drunk was embarrassing.

It was the boredom and the uncertainty of their position that made Brett drink as she did. There was nothing of the alcoholic about her. Not, at least, for a long time. They spent their time sleeping as late as possible and then drinking. That is a simple way of stating a very complicated process, and waiting for Mike's weekly allowance, which was always late, and therefore always spent and borrowed into a week or more in advance. There was nothing to do but to drink. The drinking was not done alone in their rooms. It was all at cafés and parties, and each day became a replica of the day before. There were very few differences. You had been to bed late or gone to bed early. You felt good or you felt bad. You felt like eating a little something or you couldn't face the thought of food. It had been a good party the night before or it had been a bore. Michael had behaved abominably or Michael had been a model of admirable behavior. But usually it had been a good party because alcohol, either brandy and soda, or whiskey and soda, had a tendency to make everything much better, and for a time quite all right.

If Michael had behaved well it was probably a good party, and Michael had a strong tendency to behave well. In fact you could always count on him to behave absolutely as he should until the alcoholic process had taken place, which always seemed rather like that old grammar school experiment in which a bone is dissolved in vinegar to prove it has something or other in it. Anyway the vinegar quite changed the bone and made it very unlike itself, and you could bend it back and forth, and if it were a long enough bone and you had used enough vinegar, you could even tie it into a knot.

Brett was very different from Mike about drinking. Brett had a certain grand vitality. She had her looks too. She was not supposed to be beautiful, but in a room with women who were supposed to be beautiful she killed their looks entirely. Men thought she was lovely looking, and women called her striking looking. Painters were always asking her to sit for them and that flattered her, because she herself considered that her looks were not much, and so she spent much of her waking time sitting for portraits, none of which she ever liked. She did not seem to mind how bad the painters were. The worse they were the more it amused her. It was the being asked to sit for her portrait that she liked. One painter was as good as another. Of course the best portrait painters had done her a long time before.

Brett drank much more than Mike liked, but it never dissolved her in any way. She was always clear run, generous, and her lines were always as clear. But when she had been drunk she always spoke of it as having been blind. "Weren't we blind last night, though?" It was short for blind drunk, and the curious part was that she really became, in a way, blind. Drinking, and this does not mean the odd drink, or two or three cocktails before dinner and wine at the meal, but real drinking of the sort that kills off the good drinkers because they

Gal 2—Heming's The Sun—51902—11-12-31E

are the only ones who can do it, affected Brett in three successive stages. Drinking, say, whiskey and sodas from four o'clock in the afternoon until two o'clock in the morning Breet [*sic*] first lost her power of speech and just sat and listened, then she lost her sight and saw nothing that went on, and finally she ceased to hear. And all the time any one coming into the café would never know she had been drinking. To anyone greeting her she would respond automatically, "H*u*llo, *I* say I am blind," or something of the sort.

In sleeping and in drinking, playing bridge in the afternoon, usually having her portrait painted by some socially climbing artist who knew the value of a title on a portrait, a party somewhere every night, Brett and Mike passed the time in Paris. They were rather happy. Brett was a very happy person. Then Mike had to go to England, to London to see a lawyer about something connected with the divorce Brett was trying to get, and then to Scotland to visit his people and prove by residence that he was a dutiful son, in order that, among other things, they should not stop his allowance. Brett was left alone in Paris. She had never been very good at being alone.

CHAPTER II

I DID not want to tell this story in the first person but I find that I must. I wanted to stay well outside of the story so that I would not be touched by it in any way, and handle all the people in it with that irony and pity that are so essential to good writing. I even thought I might be amused by all the things that are going to happen to Lady Brett Ashley and Mr. Robert Cohn and Michael Campbell, Esq., and Mr. Jake Barnes, But I made the unfortunate mistake, for a writer, of first having been Mr. Jake Barnes. So it is not going to be splendid and cool and detached after all. "What a pity!" as Brett used to say.

"What a pity!" was a little joke we all had. Brett was having her portrait painted by a very rich American from Philadelphia, who sent his motor-car around each afternoon to bring her from her hotel in Montparnasse up to his Montmartre studio. Along about the third sitting Brett stopped posing for a little while to have tea, and the portrait-painter asked her: "And when you get your divorce, Lady Ashley, what will you do then?"

"Marry Mike Campbell," Brett answered.

"And what will your name be then?"

"Mrs. Campbell, of course!"

"What a pity," the portrait-painter said. "What a pity!"

So my name is Jacob Barnes and I am writing the story, not as I believe is usual in these cases, from a desire for confession, because being a Roman Catholic I am spared that Protestant urge to literary production, nor to set things all out the way they happened for the good of some future generation, nor any other of the usual highly moral urges, but because I believe it is a good story.

I am a newspaper man living in Paris. I used to think Paris was the most wonderful place in the world. I have lived in it now for six years, or however long it is since 1920, and I still see its good points. Anyway, it is the only city I want to live in. They say New York is very fine but I do not care for night life. I want to live quietly and with a certain measure of luxury, and a job that I do not want to worry about. Paris provides all these things. Paris is also a lovely town to live in once you get an apartment and give up various American fetiches such as all the year round B.V.D.s and too much exercise.

In 1916 I was invalided home from a British hospital and got a job on *The Mail* in New York. I quit to start the Continental Press Association with Robert Graham, who was then just getting his reputation as Washington correspondent. We started the Continental in one room on the basis of syndicating Bob Graham's Washington dispatches. I ran the business end and the first year wrote a special war-expert service. By 1920 the Continental was the third largest feature service in the States. I told Bob Graham that rather than stay and get rich with him the Continental could give me a job in Paris. So I made the job, and I have some stock, but not as much as I ought to have, and I do not try to run the salary up too high because if it ever got up past a certain amount there would be too many people shooting at my job as European Director of the Continental Press Association. When you have a title like that, translated into French on the letter-heads, and only have to work about four or five hours a day and all the salary you want you are pretty well fixed. I write political dispatches under my own name, and feature stuff under a couple of different names, and all the trained-seal stuff is filed through our office. It is a nice job. I want to hang on to it. Like all newspaper men I have always wanted to write a novel, and I suppose, now that I am doing it, the novel will have that awful taking-the-pen-in-hand quality that afflicts newspaper men when they start to write on their own hook.

I never hung about the Quarter much in Paris until Brett and Mike showed up. I always felt about the Quarter that I could sort of take it or leave it alone. You went into it once in a while to sort of see the animals and say hello to Harold Stearns, and on hot nights in the spring when the tables were spread out over the sidewalks it was rather pleasant. But for a place to hang around it always seemed awfully dull. I have to put it in, though, because Robert Cohn, who is one of the non-Nordic heroes of this book, had spent two years there.

The Quarter is sort of more a state of mind than a geographical area. Perfectly good Quarterites live outside the actual boundaries of Montparnasse. They can live anywhere, I suppose, as long as they come to the Quarter to think. Or whatever you call it. To have the Quarter state of mind is probably the best way of putting it. This state of mind is principally contempt. Those who work have the greatest contempt for those who don't. The loafers are leading their own lives and it is bad form to mention work. Young painters have contempt for old painters, and that works both ways too. There are contemptuous critics and contemptuous writers. Everybody seems to dislike everybody else. The only happy people are the drunks, and they, after flaming for a period of days or weeks, eventually become depressed. The Germans, too, seem happy, but perhaps that is because they can only get two weeks visas to visit Paris, and so they make a party of it. The frail young men who go about together and seem to be always present, but who really leave in periodical flights for Brussels, Berlin, or the Basque coast, to return again like the birds, even more like the birds, are not gay either. They twitter a good deal, but they are not gay. The Scandinavians are the regular, hard-working residents.

Gal 3—Hemingway's The Sun—51902—11-12-31E

They are not very gay either, although they seem to have worked out a certain pleasant way of life. The only really gay person during the time I frequented the Quarter was a splendid sort of two-hundred-pound meteoric glad girl called Flossie, who had what is known as a "heart of gold," lovely skin and hair and appetite, and an invulnerability to hang-overs. She was going to be a singer, but the drink took away her voice, and she did not seem to mind particularly. This store of gladness made her the heroine of the Quarter. Anyhow, the Quarter is much too sad and dull a place to write about, and I would not put it in except that Robert Cohn had spent two years in it. That accounts for a great many things.

During these two years Robert Cohn had lived with a lady who lived on gossip, and so he had lived in an atmosphere of abortions and rumors of abortions, doubts and speculations as to past and prospective infidelities of friends, dirty rumors, dirtier reports and dirtier suspicions, and a constant fear and dread by his lady companion that he was seeing other women and was on the point of leaving her. Somehow during this time Robert Cohn wrote a novel, a first and last novel. He was the hero of it, but it was not too badly done and it was accepted by a New York publisher. There was a great deal of fantasy in it.

At that time Robert Cohn had only two friends, an English writer named Braddocks, and myself, with whom he played tennis. He beat me regularly at tennis and was very nice about it. Cohn gave the novel to Braddocks to read and Braddocks, who was very busy on something of his own and who, as the years went on, found it increasingly difficult to read the works of writers other than himself, did not read the novel, but returned it to Cohn with the remark that this was excellent stuff, some excellent stuff, but there was a part, just a small part, he wanted to talk over with Cohn some time. Cohn asked Braddocks what the part was, and Braddocks replied that it was a matter of organization, a very slight but important matter of organization. Cohn, eager to learn and with an un-Nordic willingness to accept useful criticism, pressed to know what it was.

"I'm much too busy now to go into it, Cohn. Come around to tea some time next week and we'll talk it over." Cohn insisted Braddocks keep the manuscript until they should have a chance to discuss it.

That night after dinner Braddocks called at my flat. He drank a brandy. "I say, Barnes," he said, "do me a favor. That's a good chap. Read this thing of Cohn's and tell me if it's any good. Mind you, I don't think it can be any good. But be a good chap and run through it and let me know what it's all about."

The next evening I was sitting on the terrace of the Closerie des Lilas watching it get dark. There was a waiter at the Lilas named Anton who used to give two whiskeys for the price of one whiskey owing to a dislike he had for his boss. This waiter raised potatoes in a garden outside of Paris, beyond Montrouge, and as I sat at the table with some one else, Alec Muhr I think it was, we watched the people going by in the dusk on the sidewalk, and the great slow horses going by in the dusk on the Boulevard, and the people going home from work, and the girls starting their evening's work, and the light coming out of the *bistrop* next door where the chauffeurs from the taxi line were drinking, and we asked the waiter about his potato crop, and the waiter asked about the franc, and we read the *Paris-Soir* and *l'Intransigeant*. It was very nice, and then along came Braddocks. Braddocks came along, breathing heavily and wearing a wide black hat.

"Who's that?" Alec asked.

"Braddocks," said I, "the writer."

"Good God," said Alec, who thereafter took no further part in the conversation, and does not again appear in the story.

"Hullo," said Braddocks. "May I join you?" So he joined us.

"Did you have a look at that thing of Cohn's?"

"Yes," I said. "It's a fantasy. Lot of dreams in it."

"Just as I thought," Braddocks said. "Thanks awfully."

We looked out on the Boulevard. Two girls went by.

"Pretty good-looking girls," I said.

"Do you think so?" asked Braddocks. "My word."

We looked at the Boulevard again. The waiter came and went. Braddocks was haughty with him, speaking literary French through his moustache. Along the sidewalk came a tall, gray, lantern-jawed man, walking with a tall woman wearing a blue Italian infantry cape. They looked at our table as they passed, saw no one they knew, and went on. They seemed to be looking for some one. Braddocks clapped me on the knee.

"I say, did you see me cut him? Did you see me cut him? Can't I cut people though!"

"Who is he?"

"Belloc. Hasn't a friend in the world. I say. Did you see me cut him?"

"Hilaire Belloc?"

"Belloc. Of course. He's absolutely done for. Absolutely through."

"What did you row with him about?"

"There was no row. Simply a matter of religious intolerance. Not a review in England will touch him, I tell you."

I was very impressed by this. I can see Braddock's face, his moustache, his face in the light from the Lilas window. I did not know that the literary life could become so intense. Also I had a valuable piece of information and gossip.

The next afternoon I was sitting with several people at the Café de la Paix having coffee after lunch. Along the Boulevard des Capucines came the tall, gray-looking man and the woman wearing the blue Italian infantry cape.

"There's Hilaire Belloc," I said to the people at the table. "He hasn't a friend in the world."

"Where?" asked several people eagerly.

"There," I nodded, "standing with the woman in the blue cape."

"You mean that man in the gray suit?"

"Yes," I said. "There's not a review in England who will publish him."

"Hell. That's not Belloc," the man on my right said. "That's Allister Crowley."

So I have never felt quite the same about Braddocks since, and I should avoid as far as possible putting him into this story except that he was a great friend of Robert Cohn, and Cohn is the hero.

Robert Cohn was middleweight boxing champion of Princeton. . . .

C: LETTER FROM F. SCOTT FITZGERALD TO HEMINGWAY
(FITZGERALD'S ERRORS HAVE BEEN RETAINED)

Dear Ernest: Nowadays when almost everyone is a genius, at least for awhile, the temptation for the bogus to profit is no greater than the temptation for the good man to relax (in one mysterious way or another)—not realizing the transitory quality of his glory because he forgets that it rests on the frail shoulders of professional enthusiasts. This should frighten all of us into a lust for anything honest that people have to say about our work. I've taken what proved to be excellent advice (On The B. + Damned) from Bunny Wilson who never wrote a novel (on Gatsby—change of many thousand wds) from Max Perkins who never considered writing one, and on T. S. of Paradise from Katherine Tighe (you don't know her) who had probably never read a novel before.

[This is beginning to sound like my own current work which resolves itself into laborious + sententious preliminaries].

Anyhow I think parts of *Sun Also* are careless + ineffectual. As I said yestiday (and, as I recollect, in trying to get you to cut the 1st part of 50 Grand) I find in you the same tendency to envelope or (as it usually turns out) to *embalm* in mere wordiness an anecdote or joke thats casually appealed to you, that I find in myself in trying to preserve a piece of "fine writing." Your first chapter contains about 10 such things and it gives a feeling of condescending *casuallness*

P. 1. "highly moral story"
"Brett said" (O. Henry stuff)
"much too expensive"
"something or other" (if you don't want to tell, why waste wds. saying it. See P. 23—"*9 or 14*" and "or how many years it was since 19xx" when it would take two words to say That's what youd kid in anyone else as mere "style"— mere horseshit I can't find this latter but anyhow you've not only got to write well yourself but you've also got to *not-do* to do what anyone can do and I think that there are about 24 sneers, superiorities and nose-thumbings-at-nothing that mar the whole narrative up to p. 29 where (after a false start on the introduction of Cohn) it really gets going. And to preserve these perverse and willfull non-essentials you're done a lot of writing that *honestly* reminded me of Michael Arlen

[You know the very fact that people have committed themselves to you will make them watch you like a cat. + if they don't like it creap away like one]

For example.

Pps. 1 + 2. Snobbish (not in itself but because of the history of English Aristocrats in the war, set down so verbosely so uncritically, so exteriorly and yet so obviously inspired from within, is *shopworn*.) You had the same problem that I had with my Rich Boy, previously debauched by Chambers ect. Either bring more thot to it with the realization that that ground has already raised its wheat + weeds or cut it down to seven sentences. It hasn't even your rhythym and the fact that may be "true" is utterly immaterial.

That biography from you, who allways believed in the superiority (the preferability) of the *imagined* to the *seen not to say to the merely recounted.*

P. 3 "Beautifully engraved shares"
(Beautifully engraved 1886 irony) All this is O.K. but so glib *when* its glib + *so* profuse.

P. 5 Painters are no longer *real* in prose. They must be minimized. [This is not done by making them schlptors, backhouse wall-experts or miniature painters]

P. 8. "highly moral urges" "because I believe its a good story" If this paragraph isn't maladroit then I'm a rewrite man for Dr. Cadman.

P. 9. Somehow its not good. I can't quite put my hand on it—it has a ring of "This is a true story ect."

P. 10. "Quarter being a state of mine ect." This is in all guide books. I haven't read Basil Swoon's but I have fifty francs to lose. [About this time I can hear you say "Jesus this guy thinks Im lousy. + he can stick it up his ass for all I give a Gd Dm for his 'critisism'." But remember this is a new departure for you, and that I think your stuff is great. You were the first American I wanted to meet in Europe—and the last. (This latter clause is simply to balance the sentence. It doesn't seem to make sense tho I have pawed at it for several minutes. Its like the age of the French women.

P. 14 (+ therabout) as I said yesterday I think this anecdote is flat as hell without naming Ford which would be cheap.

It's flat because you end with mention of Allister Crowly. If he's nobody it's nothing. If he's somebody, it's cheap. This is a novel. Also I'd cut out mention of H. Stearns earlier.

Why not cut the inessentials in Cohens biography? His first marriage is of no importance. When so many people can write well + the competition is so heavy I can't imagine how you could have done these first 20 pps. so casually. You can't *play* with peoples attention—a good man who has the power of arresting attention at will must be especially careful.

From here. Or rather from p. 30 I began to like the novel but Ernest I can't tell you the sense of disappointment that beginning with its elephantine facetiousness gave me. Please do what you can about it in proof. Its 7500 words—you could reduce it to 5000. And my advice is not to do it by mere pareing but to take out the worst of the *scenes*.

I've decided not to pick at anything else because I wasn't at all inspired to pick when reading it. I was much too excited. Besides This is probably a heavy dose. That novel's damn good. The central theme is marred somewhere but hell! unless you're writing your life history where you have an inevitable pendulum to swing you true (Harding metaphor), who can bring it entirely off? And what critic can trace whether the fault lies in a possible insufficient thinking out, in the biteing off of more than you eventually cared to chew in the impotent theme or in the elusiveness of the lady character herself. My theory always was that she dramatized herself in terms of Arlen's dramatization of somebody's dramatizing of Stephen McKenna's dramatization of the last girl in Well's *Tono Bungay*—who's original probably liked more things about Beatrix Esmond that about Jane Austin's Elizabeth (to whom we owe the manners of so many of our wives.)

Appropos of your foreward about the Latin quarter—suppose you had begun your stories with phrases like: "Spain is a peculiar place—ect" or "Michigan is interesting to two classes—the fisherman + the drummer."

Pps 64 + 65 with a bit of work should tell all that need be known about *Brett's* past.

(Small point) "Dysemtry" instead of "killed" is a clichês to avoid a clichê. It stands out. I suppose it can't be helped. I suppose all the 75,000000 Europeans who died between 1914-1918 will always be among the 10,000,000 who were killed in the war.

God! The bottom of p. 77 Jusque the top p. 78 are wonderful, I go crazy when people aren't always at their best. This isn't picked out—I just happened on it.

The heart of my critisism beats somewhere apon p. 87. I think you can't change it, though. I felt the lack of some crazy torturing tentativeness or security—horror, all at once, that she'd feel—and he'd feel—maybe I'm crazy. He isn't *like an impotent man. He's like a man in a sort of moral chastity belt.*

Oh, well. It's fine, from Chap V on, anyhow, in spite of that—which fact is merely a proof of its brillance.

Station Z. W. X. square says good night. Good night all.

Selected Bibliography

COLLECTIONS

The Ernest Hemingway Papers in the John F. Kennedy Library, Boston. This collection is indexed in *Catalog of the Ernest Hemingway Collection at the John F. Kennedy Library,* 2 vols. (Boston: G. K. Hall, 1982).

The Hemingway Collection in the Manuscripts Department of the Alderman Library, University of Virginia, Charlottesville.

HEMINGWAY'S PUBLISHED WORKS

Death in the Afternoon. New York: Scribner's, 1932.

A Farewell to Arms. New York: Scribner's, 1929.

For Whom the Bell Tolls. New York: Scribner's, 1940.

in our time. Paris: Three Mountains Press, 1924.

In Our Time. New York: Boni & Liveright, 1925.

A Moveable Feast. New York: Scribner's, 1964.

The Nick Adams Stories. New York: Scribner's, 1972.

The Sun Also Rises. New York: Scribner's, 1926.

Three Stories and Ten Poems. Paris and Dijon: Contact Publishing Co., 1923.

The Torrents of Spring. New York: Scribner's, 1926.

SECONDARY WORKS

Baker, Carlos. *Ernest Hemingway: A Life Story.* New York: Scribner's, 1969.

———, ed. *Ernest Hemingway: Critiques of Four Major Novels.* New York: Scribner's, 1962.

———. *Hemingway: The Writer as Artist.* Princeton, N.J.: Princeton University Press, 1952; rev., 1972.

———, ed. *Hemingway and His Critics: An International Anthology.* New York: Hill & Wang, 1961.

———. "Letters from Hemingway." *Princeton University Library Chronicle* 24 (Winter 1963): 101-7.

Baker, Sheridan. *Ernest Hemingway: An Introduction and Interpretation.* New York: Holt, Rinehart & Winston, 1967.

Benson, Jackson. *Hemingway: The Writer's Art of Self Defense.* Minneapolis: University of Minnesota Press, 1969.

———, ed. *The Short Stories of Ernest Hemingway: Critical Essays.* Durham, N.C.: Duke University Press, 1975.

Broer, Lawrence R. *Hemingway's Spanish Tragedy.* University: University of Alabama Press, 1973.

Bruccoli, Mathew, and Clark, C. E. Frazer, Jr., eds. *Fitzgerald/Hemingway Annual.* Washington: Microcard Editions, 1969.

Callaghan, Morley. *That Summer in Paris: Memories of Tangled Friendships with Hemingway, Fitzgerald and Some Others.* New York: Coward-McCann, 1963.

Donaldson, Scott. *By Force of Will: The Life and Art of Ernest Hemingway.* New York: Viking, 1977.

———. " 'Irony and Pity'—Anatole France Got It Up." In *Fitzgerald/Hemingway Annual.* Detroit: Gale Research Co., 1978.

Fenton, Charles A. *The Apprenticeship of Ernest Hemingway: The Early Years.* New York: Farrar, Straus, & Young, 1954.

Giger, Romeo. *The Creative Void: Hemingway's Iceberg Theory.* Bern: Francke, 1977.

Grebstein, Sheldon Norman. *Hemingway's Craft.* Carbondale: Southern Illinois University Press, 1973.

Gurko, Leo. *Ernest Hemingway and the Pursuit of Heroism.* New York: Crowell, 1968.

Hanneman, Audre. *Ernest Hemingway: A Comprehensive Bibliography.* Princeton, N.J.: Princeton University Press, 1967.

Hemingway, Gregory. *Papa: A Personal Memoir.* Boston: Houghton Mifflin, 1976.

Hemingway, Leicester. "Ernest Hemingway's Boyhood Reading." *Mark Twain Journal* 12 (Winter 1964): 4-5.

Hotchner, A. E. *Papa Hemingway: A Personal Memoir.* New York: Random House, 1966.

Hovey, Richard B. *Hemingway: The Inward Terrain.* Seattle: University of Washington Press, 1968.

———. *"The Torrents of Spring:* Prefigurations in the Early Hemingway." *College English* 26 (March 1965): 460–64.

Joost, Nicholas. *Ernest Hemingway and the Little Magazines: The Paris Years.* Barre, Mass.: Barre Publishers, 1968.

Kashkeen, Ivan. "What Is Hemingway's Style?" *Soviet Literature* 6 (June 1964): 172–80.

Koontz, Leah Rice. "My Favorite Subject is Hadley." *Connecticut Review* 8 (October 1974): 36–41.

Lauter, Paul. "Plato's Stepchildren, Gatsby and Cohn." *Modern Fiction Studies* 9 (Winter 1963/64): 338–46.

Loeb, Harold. "Hemingway's Bitterness." *Connecticut Review* 1 (1967): 7-24.

———. *The Way It Was.* New York: Criterion Books, 1959.

McAlmon, Robert. *Being Geniuses Together, 1920–1930.* Garden City, N.Y.: Doubleday, 1968.

McCaffery, John K. M., ed. *Ernest Hemingway: The Man and His Work.* Cleveland: World, 1950.

Miller, Madeline Hemingway. *Ernie.* New York: Crown, 1975.

Montgomery, Constance C. *Hemingway in Michigan.* New York: Fleet, 1966.

Moore, Geoffrey. "The Sun Also Rises: Notes Toward an Extreme Fiction." *Review of English Literature* 4 (October 1963): 31–46.

Moss, Sidney P. "Character, Vision and Theme in *The Sun Also Rises.*" *Iowa English Yearbook* 9 (1964): 64–67.

Oldsey, Bernard. *Hemingway's Hidden Craft: The Writing of "A Farewell to Arms."* University Park: Pennsylvania State University Press, 1979.

Peterson, Richard K. *Hemingway: Direct and Oblique.* The Hague: Mouton, 1969.

Reynolds, Michael. "False Dawn: *The Sun Also Rises* Manuscript." In *A Fair Day in the Affections: Literary Essays in Honor of Robert B. White, Jr.,* ed. Jack D. Durant and M. Thomas Hester. Raleigh, N.C.: Winston Press, 1981.

———. *Hemingway's First War: The Making of "A Farewell to Arms."* Princeton, N.J.: Princeton University Press, 1976.

Rouch, John. "Jake Barnes as Narrator." *Modern Fiction Studies* 11 (Winter 1965/66): 361–70.

Rovit, Earl. *Ernest Hemingway.* New York: Twayne, 1963.

Sarason, Bertram D. *Hemingway and the Sun Set.* Washington, D.C.: Microcard Editions, 1972.

Scott, Arthur. "In Defense of Cohn." *College English* 18 (March 1957): 309-14.

Seldes, Gilbert. "Spring Flight." *Dial* 79 (August 1925): 162–64.

Stephens, Robert O., ed. *Ernest Hemingway: The Critical Reception.* New York: Burt Franklin & Co., 1977.

Sutherland, Fraser. *The Style of Innocence: A Study of Hemingway and Callaghan.* Toronto: Clarke, Irwin & Co., 1972.

Tavernier-Courbin, Jacqueline. *Ernest Hemingway: L'éducation européenne de Nick Adams.* Paris: Didier, 1978.

Vance, William L. "Implications of Form in *The Sun Also Rises.*" In *The Twenties, Poetry and Prose: Twenty Critical Essays,* ed. Richard E. Langford and William E. Taylor. Deland, Fla.: Everett Edwards Press, 1966.

Vanderbilt, Kermit. "*The Sun Also Rises:* Time Uncertain." *Twentieth Century Literature* 15 (October 1969): 153–54.

Wagner, Linda W. *Ernest Hemingway: A Reference Guide.* Boston: G. K. Hall & Co., 1977.

———, ed. *Ernest Hemingway: Five Decades of Criticism.* East Lansing: Michigan State University Press, 1974.

———. *Hemingway and Faulkner: Inventors/Masters.* Metuchen, N.J.: Scarecrow Press, 1975.

———. "Juxtaposition in Hemingway's *In Our Time.*" *Studies in Short Fiction* 12 (Summer 1975): 243–52.

Waldhorn, Arthur. *A Reader's Guide to Ernest Hemingway.* New York: Farrar, Straus & Giroux, 1972.

Watts, Emily S. *Ernest Hemingway and the Arts.* Urbana: University of Illinois Press, 1971.

Weeks, Robert P., ed. *Hemingway: A Collection of Critical Essays.* Englewood Cliffs, N.J.: Prentice-Hall, 1962.

White, William, ed. *Byline: Ernest Hemingway.* New York: Scribner's, 1967.

———, ed. *The Merrill Checklist of Ernest Hemingway.* Columbus, Ohio: Charles E. Merrill Publishing Co., 1970.

———, ed. *The Merrill Studies in "The Sun Also Rises."* Columbus, Ohio: Charles E. Merrill Publishers, 1969.

Young, Philip. *Ernest Hemingway: A Reconsideration.* University Park: Pennsylvania State University Press, 1966.

———, and Mann, Charles. *The Hemingway Manuscripts: An Inventory.* University Park: Pennsylvania State University Press, 1969.

Index

145